Springtime of Evangelization

Springtime of Evangelization

The Complete Texts of the Holy Father's
1998 ad Limina Addresses to
the Bishops of the United States

Basilica Press
SAN DIEGO

Ignatius Press
SAN FRANCISCO

Basilica Press
Post Office Box 675205
Rancho Santa Fe, California 92067
www.basilica.com

Cover design by John A. Torres

99 00 01 02 03 15 14 13 12 11 10 09 08 07 06 05 04 03 02 01

Printed in the United States of America ∞
ISBN 0–9642610–3–0

Basilica Press is a division of the Missionaries of Faith Foundation.

Contents

5

To Pope John Paul II,
with abiding gratitude
and filial affection

Preface

"Near the cross of Jesus stood his mother, and his mother's sister, Mary the wife of Clopas, and Mary of Magdala. Seeing his mother and the disciple he loved standing near her. . ." (John 19:25–26). It was at this moment that Jesus entrusted his mother to the care of the beloved disciple. This symbolic moment represents the care that every bishop exercises when the Church is entrusted to him.

Pope John Paul II's coat of arms depicts a cross with an *M* at its foot. It represents Christ's passion and love and the compassion and suffering of the first and most faithful disciple, the Virgin Mary. This seal manifests both Christ's love and the truth of the cross, which every authentic disciple must embrace. Every bishop is himself governed by this truth lived in love in order to care for the Church. To some this is a sign of contradiction, but the bishop must be the first to follow Christ and the first to serve his people.

The *ad limina* visits of the bishops with the Successor of Peter are a privileged moment when they who have been entrusted by Christ with the care of the Church share their hopes and their anxieties with one another in service of the truth lived in love. This collection of the most recent *ad limina* talks to the bishops of the thirteen regions that make up the episcopal Conference in the United States reflect concerns born from that truth in love which is the hallmark of the collaborative dialogue between Pope and bishop.

While the general order of these talks follows that of *Gaudium et Spes*, with its emphasis on the Church as mystery and sacrament of the encounter between God and his people,[1] two themes are consistent in all the talks and should be highlighted.

The first theme is the necessary interpersonal relations among Pope, bishops, priests, laity and persons in consecrated life. No program, no administratively efficient structure, can replace the personal witness of faith that the world hungers for spiritually. Conversion, both individual and social, is a change born of a personal encounter with Christ and with his disciples.

The second theme is somewhat more specific to the United States, but not exclusively so. It deals with the relativity of truth, which so marks contemporary culture and which has several consequences. The first consequence is resistance to any objective content of religious truth; there can be only an admixture of truths that compete at various levels. The second consequence follows from this. The human conscience is considered autonomous only when it is free from any criteria greater than the judgment of conscience itself. The third consequence is that, because conscience and religion are so subjective, they are only private acts and as such have no place in the public sphere. The Pope points to the instability of a culture which sacrifices objective truth on the altar of subjective freedom, just as he contested a social system which sacrificed personal freedom on the altar of Marxist justice. How can the Church and her pastors stand by silently in public debate when the most religious and loving action in history, the passion, crucifixion and death of Jesus Christ, took place in the most public forum. At the foot of Christ's cross stand Mary and John,

---

[1] See also the *Catechism of the Catholic Church*, nn. 770–972.

the Pope and the bishops, looking at truth incarnate give up his life for love of his people. In the shadow of the cross, bishops pastor the body of Christ and help Christ's disciples transform the culture.

In collating the *ad limina* addresses of the Holy Father, Father Thomas Williams, L.C., provides a document which helps the Church continue the work of Vatican II and prepare for a New Springtime of the Gospel in the new Millennium.

— *Francis Cardinal George, O.M.I.*

Francis Cardinal George is archbishop of Chicago.

Foreword

A MOMENT CATHOLIC AND AMERICAN

What a very good idea this book is. Some may be skeptical about that. After all, there is a strong element of the pro forma in addresses such as these. There are all those bishops standing there facing the Holy Father and protocol requires that he make a little speech. It would be very awkward if they just stood there looking at one another. So he makes a little speech. Pro forma — as in formality, ritual, perfunctory ceremony. The skepticism about trying to make a book out of such addresses is understandable but, in this case, entirely unwarranted.

Over the years that I have been observing and writing about John Paul II, I have been struck by the extraordinary teaching energy of this pontificate. It is no surprise, therefore, that the Holy Father does not miss the opportunity of making the most of the *ad limina* visits as a teaching moment. I had read the individual addresses as they were published over the course of a year, but you do not really see what the Pope is saying to the bishops and to the Catholic faithful of the United States until you put the addresses together in one volume. We are all indebted to the Legion of Christ and to the editor, Father Thomas Williams, for the gift of this book.

Coming immediately before the final blessing, the very last words of the very last address (to the bishops of New England) are the Holy Father's prayer that "your country may carry out its historical destiny among the peoples of the world." The theme of American possibility and American responsibility recurs throughout these addresses, as it has been a distinctive mark of this pontificate. That was evident also at the Synod for America convoked by the Holy Father in 1997. As I noted in my book occasioned by the synod (*Appointment in Rome: The Church in America Awakening*), about one half of all the Catholics in the world are now in America — meaning North, Central, and South America — and John Paul II recognizes this as a providential convergence of the course of the Church and the course of America in world history.

He recognizes that the Church in the United States bears a most particular burden of possibility and, therefore, responsibility. The United States is, for better or worse, what social scientists call the "lead society" in world history. What happens here will, *mutatis mutandis*, happen elsewhere. This is the case in culture, economics, politics, and technology. Of all the factors that shape history, this Pope is convinced that culture is the most important. How people try to make sense of the world, how they define the good life, how they inculcate the moral visions by which they would live — this is the stuff of culture. The word "culture," we need always to be reminded, is derived from "cult." In a very deep sense, we are what we honor; we are what we worship. Of all the institutions of society, therefore, religion is the most important. This is what Tocqueville meant when, in his classic *Democracy in America*, he called religion "the first political institution" of American democracy. What he wrote in the 1830s is still true today; it is in religious communities that most Americans learn the habits of association and moral truths that make authentic politics possible. Politics, in the view of Aristotle which has been appropriated and refined in Catholic social doctrine, is the deliberation of the question, How ought we to order our life together? The "ought" in that definition makes clear that politics is essentially a moral enterprise.

Please do not misunderstand. I am not suggesting that the *ad limina* addresses in this book are about politics, at least not in the ordinary use of that term. But they are about what might be called "depth politics," which is to say they are about culture, which is to say they are about what we most solemnly honor, and finally about what we worship. For Catholics, of course, the question is *who* we worship, and the answer is we worship God, the Father, Son, and Holy Spirit. What John Paul II says about the Church in these addresses cannot be contained within the categories of the sociological or historical. The profound ecclesiology (doctrine of the Church) found here is rooted in the mystery of our *communio* with the Triune God. If we miss that great truth, we have missed the whole point of the Pope's argument.

When, for instance, he speaks about the contemplative dimension of liturgical action or about the gift of self that is the consecrated life, these questions are not unrelated to what he calls the "historical destiny" of the United States. The Holy Father's proposition with respect to what Father John Courtney Murray called "the American proposition" is that the destiny of America is inseparably joined to transcendent truth. As in the words of the Declaration of Independence, "We hold these truths to be self-evident. . . ." The Church is the bearer of the deepest truths about the human condition, upon which the truths of the American founding are radically dependent. And the deepest of the

deepest truths is none other than Jesus Christ, who *is* the
way, the truth, and the life. The Pope says here, as he has
said so often elsewhere, that Jesus Christ is the answer to
the question that is every human life. So also, Jesus Christ
is the answer to the question that is every human society.
Which means Jesus Christ is the answer to the question
that is America.

It would be a mistake, therefore, to think that some
of these addresses are about "spiritual" matters while others are about "politics," that some are about personal and
communal faith while others are about public life. The
Church is never so publicly and even politically relevant as
when we are intensely engaged in living the mystery of our
communio with God. This is what the Pope means when
he says that the Marian Church of faithful receptivity to
the grace of God has priority over the Petrine Church of
order and action. Both are necessary, of course, but without the devotion of the first the institutional power of the
second is illusory. The greatest contribution to American
public life is for Catholic Americans to live the Catholic
faith thoroughly, authentically, radically. Only in this way
is the transcendent truth proposed by which persons and
societies are both judged and renewed.

I have already mentioned John Courtney Murray. Father Murray, who died in 1967, was a Jesuit who played
a critical part in the Second Vatican Council's teaching on
democracy and religious freedom. He foresaw the day when
Catholics in America would have a most particular, even
singular, responsibility to defend and renew "the American
proposition." The day that Father Murray foresaw is now.
In the sixth address in this volume, the Holy Father tells
the American bishops: "[T]he Church continues to pro-

claim the capacity of human beings to know the truth and to grow into genuine freedom through their acceptance of that truth. In this respect, the Church is the defender of the moral insight on which your country was founded." Again in the ninth address: "Respect for the rights of conscience is deeply ingrained in your national culture, which was formed in part by emigrants who came to the New World to vindicate their religious and moral convictions in the face of persecution. American society's historic admiration for men and women of conscience is the ground on which you can teach the truth about conscience today." And so it goes throughout this book's bracing proposal to the bishops and, through the bishops, to the Catholic faithful of America.

Take note especially of what the Holy Father says about the Church's relentless emphasis upon the protection of innocent human life. The sad fact is that many Catholics, including many in public office, are embarrassed by the Church's witness on the "life questions," particularly the uncompromising witness on abortion. They say they accept Catholic doctrine as a "personal" matter but cannot "impose" their convictions on the public. This is part and parcel of the privatization of moral truth that is so effectively criticized throughout these addresses. For any society, there is no question that is more inescapably *public* than the question of who is entitled to protection in law. "This is especially important for democratic societies," says the Pope

> since one of the truths contained in the mystery of our creation by God is that the human person must be "the origin, the subject, and the purpose of all social institutions" (*Gaudium et Spes*, 25). Our intrinsic dignity and inalienable

fundamental rights are not the result of social convention: they precede all social conventions and provide the norms that determine their validity. The history of the twentieth century is a grim warning of the evils that result when human beings are reduced to the status of objects to be manipulated by the powerful for selfish gain or for ideological reasons. In proclaiming the truth that God has given men and women an inestimable dignity and inalienable rights from the moment of conception, you are helping to rebuild the moral foundations of a genuine culture of freedom, capable of sustaining institutions of self-governance that serve the common good.

In accord with this understanding of the "moral foundations" of a just and humane society, the National Conference of Catholic Bishops in November, 1998, adopted the statement, "Living the Gospel of Life." Addressed to all Catholics, and especially to those in positions of public influence, the bishops proposed the image of "the house of human dignity." For decades, Catholic Americans had spoken of abortion in the language of a "seamless garment" or of a "consistent ethic of life." Those ways of speaking were well intended, but they often led to making abortion just one more issue on a long list of issues that command moral and political attention. The phrase, "the house of human dignity," makes it unavoidably clear that the right to life is the foundation of the house. As the bishops say, there are many important issues — for instance, education, health care, racial justice, and housing — but, unless the foundation is secure, the house is built on sand.

Springtime of Evangelization is an altogether stunning proposal for the Church in the United States. I have dwelt on one aspect of the proposal: its challenge for the renewal of our public life. But this aspect is of a piece with all the other questions that the Holy Father addresses — from prayer and priesthood to new ecclesial communities and ecumenism. It is all of a piece in the Pope's compelling invitation to Catholic Americans to embrace this moment of possibility and, therefore, of responsibility to realize his prayer that "your country may carry out its historical destiny among the peoples of the world."

— Father Richard John Neuhaus

Father Neuhaus is president of the Institute on Religion and Public Life, based in New York City, and editor in chief of *First Things*. He is author of, among other books, *Appointment in Rome: The Church in America Awakening* and *The Catholic Moment: The Paradox of the Church in the Postmodern World*.

Introduction

On November 9, 1978, less than a month after his election as Bishop of Rome, Pope John Paul II had occasion to address a group of U.S. bishops for the first time as pontiff. In this very first *ad limina* discourse, John Paul spoke of his meeting with the bishops as "a celebration of the unity of the Church" and pledged "to commit my pontificate to the continued genuine application of the Second Vatican Council, under the action of the Holy Spirit."

Since then, the Pope has regularly received groups of American bishops every five years, as stipulated by Canon Law (can. 400). As in the case of his first address, John Paul has continued to stress the importance of unity among the episcopate, and invariably refers to Vatican II as the hub of his entire pontificate. He has made assiduous use of the *ad limina* visits and other such encounters to "confirm his brethren in the faith" (Cf. Luke 22:32) and to promote episcopal collegiality, as Vatican II so earnestly recommended. "Just as . . . Saint Peter and the rest of the apostles constitute a unique apostolic college," we read in *Lumen Gentium* 22, "so in like fashion the Roman Pontiff, Peter's successor, and the bishops, the successors of the apostles, are related with and united to one another."

The tradition of visits *ad limina Apostolorum* ("to the doorstep of the apostles") didn't originate with the Council, however, but goes back to early Christian times. Already in the fourth century numerous references speak of this practice. The first ecumenical councils dealt with the relationship between the local churches and the church of Rome, and in the year 597 Pope Gregory the Great recalled to his legate Cyprian the ancient custom practiced by the Sicilian bishops of visiting Rome every three years. It was Gregory who established the quinquennial visit.

In keeping with tradition, the 1983 Code of Canon Law attributes to the *ad limina* visits a threefold purpose: to venerate the tombs of Saints Peter and Paul, to meet with the Pope, and to present to the Holy Father a report on the state of the diocese. Pope John Paul has intensified these visits, and takes advantage of them to offer his brother bishops orientations and counsel in addresses which are longer and doctrinally meatier than those of his predecessors.

During the course of the year 1998, John Paul once again had the opportunity to open his mind and heart to the U.S. bishops who came to Rome to "see Peter." In this twentieth year of his pontificate the Pope delivered a series of addresses to groups of bishops representing the thirteen "ecclesiastical regions" of the United States. These brief talks grant us a privileged window into the Pope's mind. In each address the Pope tackles a different subject drawn from the major themes of the Second Vatican Council — from missionary work to the role of the laity to liturgical reform — and both the choice of topics and the manner of dealing with them tell us much about the Holy Father's thought regarding the most pressing issues facing the Church in America today.

Though the Pope delivered these talks specifically to the bishops — and frequently appeals to their personal responsibility for the flock entrusted to them — the insights and guidance he offers provide valuable orientation for all

Catholic Americans. The Holy Father's words speak to our specific situation and the difficulties and opportunities proper to the Church in the United States.

The series of talks revolves around three central themes or axes: the Great Jubilee, the new evangelization, and the application of Vatican II. In the first address John Paul made known his intention "to reflect on the opportunities presented by the Great Jubilee of the Year 2000 for *evangelization in the light of the extraordinary grace which was and is the Second Vatican Council.*"[1] Although the three themes are closely intertwined, each highlights a particular aspect of the Pope's thought and merits individual attention.

The Great Jubilee of the Year 2000

From the beginning of his pontificate, Pope John Paul II has fixed his gaze on the approaching third Christian millennium as a moment of exceptional grace. The Pope opened his very first encyclical, *Redemptor Hominis*, with a reflection on the Church at the close of the second millennium. "At this moment," he wrote back in 1979, "it is difficult to say what mark that year will leave on the face of human history. For the Church, the People of God . . . it will be the year of a great Jubilee." He compares the time of preparation for the year 2000 to "a season of a new Advent, a season of expectation" (*RH*, 1). Ever since then

---

[1] Pope John Paul II habitually underscores sections of his texts. Both in compiling the *ad limina* addresses and in citing them in this introduction, I have respected the original emphases as conveyed by the weekly English edition of *L'Osservatore Romano*.

the theme of the Jubilee has served as one of the great *leitmotivs* of John Paul's pontificate.

In his first 1998 *ad limina* address to the U.S. bishops, John Paul reiterates the hopeful message expressed in his encyclical on the missions: "We are confident that, as the Third Millennium approaches, God is preparing *a great springtime for Christianity* (cf. *Redemptoris Missio*, 86)." The Pope goes on to affirm that the Great Jubilee "will be a time of unique blessings for the Church and for the world."

Throughout the talks the Holy Father notes signs of renewal in the Church, such as an evident "thirst for God and desire for prayer," a strong and respected Catholic presence in education, and the uninterrupted growth of lay movements, which "represent a providential gift of the Holy Spirit to the Church of our time."

Yet the Pope's hopeful outlook does not stem from naivete nor from ignorance regarding the situation in the Church and in the world, but from his confidence in Christ's promise to always be with his Church and from his analysis of the real possibilities for evangelization at the present juncture in history. "At the end of the second millennium," the Pope reflects, "humanity stands at a kind of crossroads." The springtime that the Pope envisions is therefore a *project* to be realized, and not a mere fact to be taken for granted.

Thus despite his generally positive tone, the Pope doesn't conceal his deep concerns. "We are coming to the end of a century which began with confidence in humanity's prospects of almost unlimited progress," John Paul observes, "but which is now ending in widespread fear and moral confusion." Indeed, he speaks of signs of a "new spiritual crisis" and warns that if this crisis deepens, "a new era of barbarism, rather than a springtime of hope, may well follow this century of tears."

The expressions of this crisis in American society are manifold. An especially worrisome characteristic of modern culture, to which the Pope returns again and again, is the widespread phenomenon of skepticism. The Pope speaks of a cultural climate in the United States "many of whose most powerful elements doubt the existence of objective, absolute truth." This skepticism is particularly acute in the area of morality, and reveals itself in modernity's understanding of moral conscience as autonomous.

The desire for personal moral autonomy goes hand in hand with "a weakening of the sense of the innate dependence of all human existence on the Creator." Thus, John Paul continues, "the spiritual crisis of our times is in fact a flight from the transcendent mystery of God. . . . The culture of our day seeks to build without reference to the architect." Yet, this flight from the Creator is at the same time "a flight from the truth about the human person, God's noblest creation on earth."

For John Paul, one's attitude towards the value of human life marks a watershed between the believer and secular culture. Nowhere is the contrast between the Gospel vision and contemporary culture more obvious than in *"the dramatic conflict between the culture of life and the culture of death."* The Pope speaks of contemporary culture's temptation to reduce life to a commodity and exhorts his fellow bishops to "make every effort to ensure that there is *no dulling of consciences regarding the seriousness of the crime of abortion."* He also warns against other symptoms of society's erroneous approach to human life, such as euthanasia, physician-assisted suicide, ever increasing recourse to *in vitro* fertilization, and certain forms of genetic manipulation and embryo experimentation.

Besides these cultural maladies, John Paul also warns against polarization and a partisan spirit among Catholics themselves. He wonders aloud whether Catholics have sometimes "succumbed to the temptation, widespread in modern western culture, to judge the Church in predominantly political terms." John Paul challenges his brother bishops to overcome this polarization through clear, unambiguous teaching. The truth given to the Church by Christ is neither "liberal" nor "conservative"; it is simply *true*. Thus an essential part of the episcopal ministry must be to help all sectors of the Catholic community "find greater certainty about what the Church actually teaches, and greater serenity in confronting the many issues which — often needlessly — cause division and polarization among those who should be of one mind and heart (cf. Acts 2:44)."

Bearing in mind all these factors, both positive and negative, the Pope demonstrates an unflagging conviction that we are experiencing an authentic "Catholic moment," and that the end of the second Christian millennium presents unique opportunities to preach Jesus Christ and the integral truth of the Catholic faith.

"The challenge is enormous," John Paul announces in one of his more ardent appeals, *"but the time is right.* For other culture-forming forces are exhausted, implausible, or lacking in intellectual resources adequate to satisfy the human yearning for genuine liberation." The Church has much to propose, and asks only to be heard.

Opportunities for Evangelization

The heart of the Church's proposal is the person of Jesus Christ. "The two-thousandth anniversary of the birth of the Savior," the Pope proclaims, "invites the whole Church to be *absorbed with bringing Christ to the world.*" The true solution to the crises afflicting our world lies in evangelizing, in preaching Christ to our contemporaries. Pope John Paul unabashedly affirms that "genuine hope for the future of the human family lies in presenting clearly to the world the incarnate Son of God as the exemplar of all human life." Although the Holy Father touches on numerous subjects in the course of these talks, he continually returns to the theme of the new evangelization as a sort of linchpin of the entire series.

In addressing the U.S. bishops, Pope John Paul poses the double question "What is the greatest challenge before us as Bishops of the Church? What is the greatest need of our contemporaries?" He responds that our contemporaries, like those of every generation, yearn for salvation. The great truth to be proclaimed to this and every age is that "God has entered human history so that men and women can truly become children of God." The mission of proclaiming this truth forms the crux of the new evangelization. In fact, the Pope proclaims that "[*n*]*o demand on our ministry is more urgent than the 'new evangelization' needed to satisfy the spiritual hunger of our times.*"

"*The moment is right for kerygma,*" John Paul insists. "The pastoral challenge of the Great Jubilee is to proclaim with renewed vigor '*Jesus Christ, the one Savior of the world, yesterday, today and for ever*' (cf. Heb. 13:8)." The Holy Fa-

ther seems to repeat the exhortation with which he began
his pontificate: "Be not afraid!" The time is right to preach
Jesus Christ to men and women who hunger for the message of truth, for authentic liberation, for salvation. Christ
is the only answer to the deepest needs and longings of the
human person. Indeed, Pope John Paul characterizes the
present moment as evangelization's "hour."

This mission does not only involve Church "professionals," such as priests and religious. The Pope reminds his
hearers that "all baptized Christians must commit themselves to evangelization," cooperating with the work of the
Holy Spirit in the minds and hearts of all people. This
cooperation is not merely an external project. While comprising planning and hard work, it is an eminently spiritual
endeavor and the motivating force behind our evangelizing
efforts must necessarily stem from "love for Christ and a
desire to make him better known."

In the same way, the sacraments play an essential part
in the work of evangelizing, and the Pope encourages his
brother bishops to ensure "correct and worthy celebration
of the Eucharist," as well as promoting Eucharistic adoration and frequent recourse to the sacrament of Penance.
John Paul likewise recalls that evangelical witness is the
fruit of prayer. "If we are to be effective teachers," he affirms, "we must allow our entire existence to be transformed by prayer and the continuous submission of ourselves to God in imitation of Christ himself."

Since the bishop has a *personal responsibility* to teach
the faith, "he needs time to assimilate the content of the
Church's tradition and Magisterium prayerfully." Indeed,
authentic renewal may mean that the bishop will have to
"re-organize the way in which he exercises his episcopal

office in order to attend to what is fundamental in his ministry." Echoing some of the reflections made in the 1997 Synod for America, John Paul invited his brother bishops "to become more simple, with the simplicity of Jesus and of the Gospel — a simplicity which consists in being immersed in the essential things of the Father."

Catholic education is itself an essentially evangelizing enterprise, and "cannot be separated from the Lord's mandate to *preach the Gospel* to all nations." By a quaint stroke of providence the Pope chose to address his words on Catholic education to the bishops of the region comprising the birthplace of the 1967 "Land O' Lakes Document," which marked a split of Catholic higher education from the Catholic hierarchy. In so doing, John Paul does not mince words concerning the gravity of the situation. "Few areas of Catholic life in the United States," the Pope affirms, "need the leadership of the Bishops for their re-affirmation and renewal as much as this one does."

The Pope sees the most formidable challenge facing Catholic education in the United States today as restoring to our culture *"the conviction that human beings can grasp the truth of things, and in grasping that truth can know their duties to God, to themselves and their neighbors."* This is also "the greatest contribution that authentically Catholic education can make to American culture." Catholic universities are uniquely equipped to engage the current moral and intellectual crises, and in so doing can play an effective role in the renewal of both higher education and culture in the United States.

Indeed, at a time when the relationship between freedom and moral truth is being debated on a host of issues, "Catholic scholars have the resources to contribute to an intellectual and moral renewal of American culture." The Pope challenges Catholic universities to be in the forefront of "a new and long-overdue dialogue between the empirical sciences and the truths of faith." But in order to rise to this occasion, Catholic universities must be true to their character. If Catholic universities are truly to become leaders in the renewal of higher education, the Holy Father insists, "they must first have a strong sense of their own Catholic identity." This specific identity of the Catholic university "should be evident in its curriculum, in its faculty, in student activities, and in the quality of its community life."

Important as the renewal of education is, however, opportunities for evangelization do not occur exclusively or even chiefly on the institutional level. The new evangelization that can make the twenty-first century a springtime of the Gospel, the Holy Father proposes, "will depend in a decisive way on the lay faithful being fully aware of their baptismal vocation and their responsibility for bringing the good news of Jesus Christ to their culture and society." The Council did not invent the lay apostolate, but it did give it a decisive push. The Pope sees positive signs that this lay involvement continues to flourish in America. He states that "everywhere in the Church, and not least in your country, we see the spread of *a fresh and invigorating lay spirituality* and the magnificent fruits of the laity's greater involvement in the Church's life."

This increasing involvement should give birth to a more vigorous lay witness in the world, "not a confusion of roles in the worshiping community." Participation in the life and mission of the Church goes well beyond particular functions in liturgical services. Recalling the 1987 Synod on the Laity, Pope John Paul stressed that "it is an inadequate understanding of the role of the laity which leads lay men and women to become so strongly interested in Church services and tasks that they fail to become actively involved in their responsibilities in the professional, social, cultural and political field." Lay people are at the forefront of the Church's mission to evangelize all areas of human activity — including the workplace, the worlds of science and medicine, the world of politics, and the diverse world of culture — and the "first requirement of the new evangelization is *the actual witness of Christians who live by the Gospel*."

On the path marked by the Second Vatican Council

The opportunities for evangelization occasioned by the Great Jubilee form a continuum with the renewal sought by the Second Vatican Council. In line with his encyclical *Tertio Millennio Adveniente* Pope John Paul expressly proposes a "serious meditation on how we as Bishops have received and implemented the rich body of teaching elaborated by the Council Fathers (cf. *TMA*, 36)." This examination serves not only to evaluate what has been accomplished up to the present, but also "to discern how best we can ensure that all that God wishes for the Church will become a reality."

Closer attention to the Council's teaching thus provides the surest path to take full advantage of the Catholic moment heralded by the Great Jubilee. "The Council was a gift of the Holy Spirit to the Church," the Pope observes, "and its full implementation is the best means of ensuring that the Catholic community in the United States enters the new millennium strengthened in faith and holiness." In the context of this pro-active approach the Pope offers advice and directives as to how the teaching of the Council can better be applied in the United States.

The themes of the individual *ad limina* talks often correspond to specific documents or key issues addressed by Vatican II, whose fruits, beginning with the Dogmatic Constitution on Divine Revelation, *Dei Verbum*, and continuing through Conciliar documents on the Church, missions, the priesthood, and so on. Thus the basic framework of the addresses is built around the main topics dealt with by Vatican II.

Reminiscing on his own experience of the Council, the Pope recalls it as "a time of extraordinary spiritual dynamism and growth." The graces were manifold. "The Council brought us into close and tangible contact with the wealth of nineteen centuries of holiness, doctrine and service to the human family; it revealed to us the unity and diversity of the Catholic community throughout the world; it taught us openness to our Christian brothers and sisters, to the followers of other religions, to mankind's joys and hopes, griefs and anxieties." Yet the Council was a blessing not only for those who had the privilege to participate in it. Rather God, in his Providence, clearly "wanted to prepare the Church for a new springtime of the Gospel — for the beginning of the next Christian Millennium — *through the extraordinary grace of the Council*."

The Holy Father devotes considerable time to the question of the Church, and especially her own understanding of herself. In this regard, the documents of the Council "represent the fundamental point of reference for the Church's understanding of herself and her mission in this period of history," the Pope observes. He expresses concern regarding tendencies towards a reductive understanding of the Church, which have resulted in "inadequate ecclesiologies, radically different from what the Council and the subsequent Magisterium have presented."

"What must be done," the Pope asks, "to ensure that the whole Church enters the next Millennium with a clearer awareness of her own *mystery?*" He proceeds to offer a rich reflection on the reality of the Church as communion, which he describes as "the very heart of the Church's understanding of herself." For the same reason, the whole purpose of the bishops' ministry is "to lead others into this communion, which is not of our own making."

Concerning the renewal of the priesthood envisioned by the Council, the Pope spoke at length about the identity of the priest, a vocation which consists in being "uniquely *configured to Christ the High Priest, the teacher, sanctifier and shepherd of his people.*" The priest's whole life undergoes a transformation "so that he may *be Christ* for others: a convincing and efficacious sign of God's loving and saving presence." Therefore the priesthood is not a career, nor does it mean belonging to a clerical caste. Rather, the priest should live out his vocation as "*a total gift of himself to the Lord,*" which embraces every aspect of his life. Priests should be men of prayer, and men of the Eucharist. "The celebration of the Eucharist," the Holy Father reflects, "is the most important moment of the priest's day, the center of his life."

John Paul underscores the importance of the bishop as promoter of priestly vocations. "Experience has shown," the Pope observes, "that when the local Bishop takes this

responsibility seriously, there is no 'vocation shortage.'"
Young men want to be called to radical self-giving, and
the challenge of accepting Christ's call to follow him and
become "fishers of men" (Matt. 4:19). Priests play an essential role in this task as well, since for promoting vocations
"there is no substitute for the presence of a committed, mature and happy priest with whom young people can meet
and talk."

Consecrated life, too, awaits further renewal after a difficult period in its history. The Pope speaks of the period
following Vatican II as a time of adjustment "characterized
by change and adaptation" in which it has not always been
easy "to strike a proper balance between necessary change
and fidelity to the spiritual and canonical experience which
had become a stable and fruitful part of the Church's living
tradition."

Renewal implies the rediscovery of the richness of consecrated life. In a beautiful expression John Paul asserts that
consecrated persons have the "extraordinary privilege . . .
to *'be holiness' in the heart of the Church*." At the approach
of the new millennium, the Church urgently needs a vital
and attractive religious life that *"shows forth concretely the
sovereignty of God* and bears witness before the world to
*the transcendent value of the 'total gift of self in the profession
of the evangelical counsels' (Vita Consecrata,* 16)."

In a particularly powerful talk addressed to the bishops of the Northwestern United States, the Pope tackles
the question of liturgical renewal, "so vigorously promoted
by the Second Vatican Council as the prime agent of the
wider renewal of Catholic life." Drawing from the experience of more than thirty years since the publication of

the Conciliar document on the liturgy, *Sacrosanctum Concilium*, the Pope assesses both the strengths and weaknesses of the changes that have come about since the Council, and highlights key areas of work for the future.

He begins by giving thanks to God for the "marvelous awareness which has developed among the faithful of their role and responsibility in this priestly work of Christ and his Church." At the same time he recognizes that "not all changes have always and everywhere been accompanied by the necessary explanation and catechesis" sometimes resulting in "a misunderstanding of the very nature of the liturgy, leading to abuses, polarization, and sometimes even grave scandal."

In a profound reflection on the sense of the liturgy, the Holy Father explains why it is so important that the liturgical law be respected, since the liturgy transcends worshipers "as *the priestly act of Christ himself*, to which he associates us but which ultimately does not depend upon us (*SC*, 7)." The priest, as "the servant of the liturgy, not its inventor or producer," has a particular responsibility, "lest he empty liturgy of its true meaning or obscure its sacred character."

Preaching and homiletics, too, stand in need of renewal. The Pope makes particular mention of the need for contact with the Fathers of the Church as an invaluable aid to effect this renewal. Priests and deacons should be trained to make good use of the Bible, but should also be familiar "with the whole Patristic, theological and moral tradition," to avoid giving the impression "of a teaching without roots and without the universal application inherent in the Gospel message." Indeed, the Holy Father remarks, "*it is hard to imagine that there can be an effective renewal of Catholic preaching, as the Council wished, without sufficient familiarity with the Patristic tradition."*

A message for our times

Although these *ad limina* addresses were given at different times and to different groups of bishops, they can be taken as a single message to the Church in America. At the heart of the message we encounter Pope John Paul's steadfast conviction that the special graces of the Jubilee celebrations and the convergence of a series of factors, most notably the Second Vatican Council, contribute to making the present moment one of tremendous opportunity for the Church, a veritable springtime of evangelization.

While in many regards the appearance of winter lingers, unmistakable signs of new life bud forth, often where we least expect them. As in the case of springtime in nature, much work is required in order to reap the fruits. Old weeds must be uprooted; clods of cold earth must be broken up; seed must be sown; new sprouts must be cared for and protected. Thankfully the Holy Father doesn't leave Catholic Americans guessing as to where to begin hoeing. He offers numerous practical guidelines and directives to bring the project of the new evangelization to fulfillment. In the end, the harvest will be rich.

— Father Thomas D. Williams, L.C.

Father Williams is rector of the Generalate House of the Legionaries of Christ in Rome and author of *Building on Solid Ground*.

I

God's Self-Revelation to Humanity

Your Eminence,
Dear Brother Bishops,

1. Beginning this series of *ad limina* visits of the *Pastors of the Church in the United States*, I cordially welcome you, the first group of Bishops — from *the ecclesiastical region of New York* — and I send warm greetings to all the members of the Bishops' Conference. In meeting you, my first thought is to give heartfelt praise to God for the Catholic community in your country as you seek to be ever more subject to the Lord in love and fidelity (cf. Eph. 5:24), pressing forward amid the trials of this world and the consolations of God, announcing the saving cross and death of the Lord until he comes (cf. 1 Cor. 11:26). In particular I express my thanks to you and your brother Bishops for the spiritual friendship and the communion in faith and love which unite us in the service of the Gospel. I thank you for all the ways in which you share my pastoral concern for the universal Church. All through the years of my Pontificate I have had countless opportunities to experience the characteristic love and solidarity of the Catholics of the United States for the Successor of Saint Peter. In this year of preparation for the Great Jubilee, dedicated to the Holy Spirit, I pray that "the Lord, the giver of life" will reward

the Church in the United States with his strengthening
and consoling gifts.

2.   The Jubilee calls us to remember and celebrate *the
blessings that the Father has showered upon us in Jesus Christ*,
the Lord of history and the "chief shepherd" of our souls
(cf. 1 Pet. 5:4). Freed from sin and washed in the blood of
the Lamb, we have truly become children of God, able to
turn to him in absolute confidence: for we know that he
loves us and will never abandon us. Although our ministry
constantly reminds us of the sufferings of so many of our
fellow human beings, especially the poor and those who are
persecuted for their faith in Christ, we are confident that,
as the Third Millennium approaches, God is preparing *a
great springtime for Christianity* (cf. *Redemptoris Missio*, 86).

Through the Incarnation of the Son of God, eternity
has entered into time. Time itself has become the dramatic
arena in which the history of salvation unfolds; thus an-
niversaries and jubilees become times of grace — "a day
blessed by the Lord," "a year of the Lord" (cf. *Tertio Millennio Adveniente*, 32). The Great Jubilee of the Year 2000
will be a time of unique blessings for the Church and for
the world, a grace already prepared by that extraordinary
ecclesial event of recent times, the Second Vatican Council,
the fruits of which are still maturing towards their fullness.
Since the documents of the Council represent the fundamental point of reference for the Church's understanding
of herself and her mission in this period of history, it is
fitting that our preparation for the Jubilee should involve
a serious meditation on how we as Bishops have received
and implemented the rich body of teaching elaborated by
the Council Fathers (cf. *Tertio Millennio Adveniente*, 36).

In my meetings this year with the Bishops of the United States I propose to reflect on certain themes of the Council, in an effort to discern how best we can ensure that all that God wishes for the Church will become a reality.

3. What is the greatest challenge before us as Bishops of the Church? What is the greatest need of our contemporaries? The men and women of today, like those of every time and place, are yearning for salvation. They wish *to rediscover the truth of God's dominion over creation and history, to encounter his self-revelation, and to experience his merciful love in all the dimensions of their lives.* The great truth to be proclaimed to this and every age is that God has entered human history so that men and women can truly become children of God. The Dogmatic Constitution on Divine Revelation, *Dei Verbum*, clearly reminds us that *the truth we proclaim is no human wisdom, but depends completely on God's revelation of himself*: "God chose to reveal himself and to make known to us the hidden purpose of his will by which through Christ, the Word made flesh, man has access to the Father in the Holy Spirit and comes to share in the divine nature" (*op. cit.*, 2). This is the heart of the Christian message and *the essential truth which Bishops must preach "in season and out of season"* (2 Tim. 4:2).

In the Apostolic Letter *Tertio Millennio Adveniente*, I posed the question: "*To what extent has the word of God become more fully the soul of theology and the inspiration of the whole of Christian living as Dei Verbum sought?*" (no. 36). From everyone, but especially from the Bishops, fidelity to the revealed word requires an attitude of attentive, prayerful receptivity. It requires that we allow ourselves to be renewed and transformed by our encounter with his living

word. Then we will be able to help the faithful to understand that Holy Scripture is *a gift which we receive within
the Church*. It is not merely a "text" to be analyzed; it is
above all an invitation to communion with the Lord. It
must be read and received in a spirit of openness to that
invitation. This does not imply an uncritical approach to
Scripture, but it does warn against readings informed by a
sterile rationalism or by cultural pressures that compromise
biblical truth. These approaches close the ear to God's call
and empty the sacred text of its power to save (cf. Rom.
1:16). Saint Paul gives thanks to God for those who have
accepted Scripture for what it really is: the word of God
at work in the community of believers (cf. 1 Thess. 4:13).

Tribute must be paid to the many excellent *Catholic
exegetes and theologians* in the United States who have been
untiring in their efforts to help the Christian people to understand more clearly the word of God in Scripture, "so
that they can better accept [it] in order to live in full communion with God" (*Address on the Interpretation of the Bible
in the Church*, 23 April 1993, no. 9). This important work
will bear the fruit the Council intended if it is sustained by
a vigorous spiritual life within the believing community.
Only the love that "issues from a pure heart and a good
conscience and sincere faith" (1 Tim. 3:5) enables us to understand the language of God who is Love (cf. 1 John 4:8).

4. If *the new evangelization* is to be effective, our catechesis must convey the full truth of the Gospel, for that
fullness of truth is the very source of our capacity to teach
with authority: an authority which the faithful easily recognize when we *address the essentials and deliver what we
have received* (cf. 1 Cor. 15:3). Our teaching office "is not

above the word of God but serves it, teaching only what has been handed on, listening to it devoutly (*pie audit*), guarding it scrupulously (*sancte custodit*) and explaining it faithfully (*fideliter exponit*) by divine commission and with the help of the Holy Spirit" (*Dei Verbum*, 10).

Through the ministry of preaching and teaching, the whole believing community must come to see and to love Scripture and Tradition, which together lead us to understand God's salvific presence in history and show the path to real communion of life with him. In this way the entire Church will enter more deeply into the mystery of salvation, and will come to appreciate that *human history is the place of encounter between God and man, the place in which communion with God is offered, received and built up.*

5. The Gospel message remains ever the same, yet we proclaim it in a culture which is undergoing constant transformation. We need to reflect on the dynamics of contemporary culture in order to discern the signs of the times which affect the proclamation of the saving message of Christ. On the one hand, everywhere we see people's desire for freedom and happiness, and this speaks to us of *a deep spiritual hunger*. People seek to satisfy this hunger in many ways; but the failure of many proposed solutions, be they philosophies, ideologies or fashions, has led to a great unease, if not a current of despair, in contemporary culture. Ours is often called a time of uncertainty; this uncertainty, raised to a principle by which it is denied that we can ever know the truth of things, affects the moral life, the life of prayer, and the theological correctness of people's faith (cf. *Tertio Millennio Adveniente*, 36).

On the other hand, many people are increasingly aware

that, in order to build free, just, and prosperous societies
and so create the conditions for satisfying the deepest and
noblest aspirations of the human spirit, the culture through
which they interact and communicate must *correspond to
certain basic truths about the human person*. My last visit to
your country took place in 1995, during the fiftieth anniversary celebration of the United Nations Organization.
At the General Assembly I expressed the conviction that
an acceleration of the human quest for freedom is one of
the great dynamics of modern history in every part of the
world. That dynamic shows itself clearly in the claims of
the world's peoples for a fuller share in determining the
political and economic choices which affect them (cf. *Address to the Fiftieth General Assembly of the United Nations
Organization*, October 5, 1995, no. 2). In the unfolding of
history, do we not see the gradual advance of certain Gospel
truths: the dignity of the human person, greater respect for
human rights, an overdue recognition of the equal dignity
of women, a rejection of violence as a means of resolving
conflict?

6. But the affirmation of certain moral values is not
yet *the proclamation of Jesus Christ, the one mediator between
God and men* (cf. 1 Tim. 2:5). Our age needs to hear the revealed truth about God, about man, and about the human
condition. *The moment is right for kerygma*. The pastoral
challenge of the Great Jubilee is to proclaim with renewed
vigor *"Jesus Christ, the one Savior of the world, yesterday, today
and for ever"* (cf. Heb. 13:8). And the Catholic community
in the United States is called to do so in a cultural climate,
many of whose most powerful elements doubt the existence
of objective, absolute truth and reject the very idea of au-
thoritative teaching. The challenge of radical skepticism

can lead to the assumption that the Church is marginal to contemporary life. Accepting this assumption, in turn, can lead to the notion that Catholicism, and indeed Christianity as a whole, is merely one form among many of the generic human reality called "religion."

This is not the message of the Second Vatican Council, which boldly proclaimed *the centrality for human history of Jesus Christ* and the essential mission of the Church to preach the Gospel to all nations: for "there is no other name under heaven given to man by which he must be saved" (Acts 4:12). The Church is *sent* to the world with a *proposal*: and the evangelical proposal we make is that the world can understand its history and its aspirations most adequately, most *truthfully*, through the Gospel. If this is the truth we proclaim, then the Church is never marginal, even when she seems weak in the eyes of the world. Faced with a *modernity* which has lost the capacity to fulfill the noble aspiration it set out to realize — *the complete liberation of man*, of every man and every woman — the Church remains a witness to the full meaning of human freedom. A new phase in the history of freedom is opening up, and in these circumstances it is necessary that the Church, especially through her Pastors, teach and evince that "the liberating capacities of science, technology, work, economics and political activity will only produce results if they find their inspiration and measure in the truth and love which are stronger than suffering: the truth and love revealed to men by Jesus Christ" (Congregation for the Doctrine of the Faith, *Instruction on Christian Freedom and Liberation*, March 22, 1986, no. 24).

The challenge is enormous, but the time is right. For other culture-forming forces are exhausted, implausible, or lacking in intellectual resources adequate to satisfy the human yearning for genuine liberation — even if those forces still manage to exercise a powerful attraction, especially through the media. The great achievement of the Council is to have positioned the Church to engage *modernity* with the truth about the human condition, given to us in Jesus Christ who is the answer to the question that is every human life. A Bishop's task is none other than this: *to be a convincing witness to and a courageous teacher of the truth that makes man free* (cf. John 8:42).

7. Dear Brother Bishops: at the Last Supper, Jesus challenged and encouraged his disciples: "If anyone loves me he will keep my word, and my Father will love him, and we shall come to him and make our home with him" (John 14:23). We know that the Spirit dwells in the midst of the Church and leads the faithful to an ever more profound understanding of God's word, because Christ told his disciples that the Spirit "will teach you everything and remind you of all I have said to you" (John 14:26). May the Spirit always assist you in fulfilling the task which the Council committed above all to the Church's Pastors: that of *communicating the truth and grace of Christ to the men and women of today's world* (cf. *Ad Gentes*, 2; *Redemptoris Missio*, 1). I commend to the intercession of Mary, Mother of the Church and Patroness of the United States, the joys and difficulties of your ministry and the needs and hopes of your local Churches and of the whole Catholic community in your country. To each of you and to all the priests, religious and laity of your Dioceses, I cordially impart my Apostolic Blessing.

— From the Vatican, February 27, 1998

II

The Mystery of the Church

Dear Cardinal Bevilacqua,
Dear Brother Bishops,

1. "Grace to you and peace from God our Father and the Lord Jesus Christ" (Rom. 1:7). Continuing this series of *ad limina* visits by the Bishops of the United States, I welcome you, *the Bishops of Pennsylvania and New Jersey*. I entrust the outcome of our prayer and meetings to the grace of the Holy Spirit, who "down through the centuries has drawn from the treasures of the Redemption achieved by Christ and given new life to human beings" (*Dominum et Vivificantem*, 53). The Spirit is now preparing the Church for the Great Jubilee, a time to hear anew and answer ever more decisively the call to open our hearts to the Gospel, to embrace its saving message, and to allow it to transform our lives. Approaching the Jubilee, the Shepherds of God's people have a fresh opportunity to speak out and tell the men and women of today that God has indeed come among us and that the Gospel is "the power of God for salvation to every one who has faith" (Rom. 1:16). Let us pray that the Holy Spirit will further *enlighten our minds regarding the "hour" that we are living* and regarding the opportunities and responsibilities which this "hour" entails for the future of the Church and of society.

2. As I mentioned to the first group of Bishops from your country, the reception given to the teachings of the *Second Vatican Council*, and the renewal of the Church envisioned by the Council, will be the guiding light of our reflections during this series of visits *ad limina Apostolorum*. Many Catholics today have no personal recollection of the Council. But those of us who had the marvelous opportunity to take part in it experienced it as a time of extraordinary spiritual dynamism and growth. The Council brought us into close and tangible contact with the wealth of nineteen centuries of holiness, doctrine and service to the human family; it revealed to us the unity and diversity of the Catholic community throughout the world; it taught us openness to our Christian brothers and sisters, to the followers of other religions, to mankind's joys and hopes, griefs and anxieties. It is clear that in his Providence, God wanted to prepare the Church for a new springtime of the Gospel — for the beginning of the next Christian Millennium — *through the extraordinary grace of the Council.*

Among the teachings which the Council has bequeathed to us, none has had so far-reaching an influence on the Catholic community as a whole, and on our own lives as priests and Bishops, as *the Church's reflection on herself, ad intra* and *ad extra*, in the Dogmatic Constitution on the Church *Lumen Gentium* and the Pastoral Constitution on the Church in the Modern World *Gaudium et Spes*. How deeply has the Council's vision of the Church penetrated the life of our Christian communities? What must be done to ensure that the whole Church enters the next Millennium with a clearer awareness of her own *mystery*, with fuller confidence in her unique importance for the human family, with ardent commitment to her mission?

3. As Bishops, we have an urgent responsibility to help God's people to understand and appreciate *the profound mystery of the Church:* to see her above all as *the community in which we meet the living God and his merciful love.* It must be our pastoral objective to create a more intense awareness of the fact that God, who intervenes in history at times of his choosing, in the fullness of time sent his Son, born of a woman, for the salvation of the world (cf. Gal. 4:4). This is the great truth of human history: that *the history of salvation has entered the history of the world,* making it a history filled with God's presence and punctuated by events overflowing with meaning for the people God calls to be his own. The redemptive work of the Son continues in the Church and through the Church. Indeed, from the beginning God "planned to assemble in the Holy Church all those who would believe in Christ" (*Lumen Gentium,* 2). In this transcendent, theological sense, *the Church is the goal of all things*: for God created the world in order to communicate his own infinite goodness and to draw his beloved creatures into communion with himself, a communion brought about by the *convocation* of all in Christ. *This convocation is the Church* (cf. *Catechism of the Catholic Church,* 760). "Just as God's will is creation and is called 'the world', so his intention is the salvation of men, and it is called 'the Church'" (Clement of Alexandria, *Paedagogus,* I, 6, 27).

4. The fundamental truth about the Church which the Council Fathers sought to underline is that she is "the kingdom of Christ now present in mystery" (*Lumen Gentium,* 3). Christ's disciples are "in the world" without being "of the world" (John 17:16); so they are obviously affected by

the economic, social, political and cultural processes which determine how peoples and societies live and act. Thus, on her pilgrim journey through history, the Church adapts to changing circumstances while always remaining the same, in fidelity to her Lord, to his revealed word and to "what has been handed on" under the guidance of the Holy Spirit. In the post-conciliar period we have been called to serve God's people in the midst of profound social change. The rapidity of change in the thirty years since the Council, and the tendency of western cultures to confine religious convictions within the private sphere, has made it difficult in some cases for Catholics to "receive" the Council's teaching on the Church's unique nature and mission. The cultural history of the United States has had a particular impact on how Catholics have perceived the Church in recent decades. It is necessary to remind everyone that, precisely because the Church is a "mystery," her reality can never be fully captured by sociological or political categories or analyses.

Following the lead of Pope Pius XII in his Encyclical *Mystici Corporis*, and after a period in which ecclesiology tended to focus primarily on the Church as an institution, the Second Vatican Council sought to deepen appreciation of *the Church as the sacrament of encounter with the living Christ*. As Shepherds of souls, we must ask ourselves to what degree the call of *Lumen Gentium* to a more profound sense of the interior mystery of the Church has been heard. Or have Catholics sometimes succumbed to the temptation, widespread in modern western culture, to judge the Church in predominantly political terms? It was surely not the Council's intention to "politicize" the Church so that every issue became susceptible to a political label. On the contrary, it was precisely to broaden and deepen our faith in and experience of the Church as a communion that the Council Fathers described the Church through that marvelous array of Biblical images we find in *Lumen Gentium* 5 and 6, rather than in the institutional categories to which they were accustomed.

Now, more than thirty years after *Lumen Gentium* and *Gaudium et Spes*, we have sufficient perspective to see that while *the fruits of the Council are manifold and everywhere there are signs that the Council has brought a new steadfastness in the faith, new signs of holiness, and a new love of the Church*, there are still some tendencies towards a reductive understanding of the Church. As a result, inadequate ecclesiologies, radically different from what the Council and the subsequent Magisterium have presented, have found their way into theological and catechetical works. In pastoral practice these have become the basis of a more or less horizontal and sociological view of ecclesial realities on the part of some sectors of Catholicism. We must, therefore, look again at our efforts to teach the richly-textured ecclesiology of the Council.

5. We can only truly appreciate what the Church is when we understand that every aspect of her being is shaped by the new relationship, the new covenant, which God established between himself and mankind through the Cross of Christ. The mystery which envelops us is a mystery of communion, a sharing through grace in the life of the Father given us through Christ in the Holy Spirit. We should never cease to reflect on the call to enter into this intimate relationship of life and love with the Most Blessed Trinity. The whole purpose of our ministry is to

lead others into this communion, which is not of our own
making. We have to lead the faithful to understand that
we do not enter into communion with God simply through
a personal option in accordance with our private tastes; we
do not join the Church as we join some voluntary association. Rather, we are incorporated into the Body of Christ
through the grace of Baptism and through full participation in all that constitutes the divine-human reality of the
Church.

The community of Christ's followers is therefore above
all a spiritual solidarity, the *communio sanctorum*. We are
the pilgrim People of God, journeying to our heavenly
home, assisted by the intercession of Mary and the Saints
who have preceded us. The Church embraces those who
now see God as he is, and those who have died and are
being purified. Perhaps our consciousness of this dimension
of the Church's nature has decreased somewhat in recent
years. More attention needs to be given to the intimate relationship between the Church on earth and the Church
in heaven. Are younger Catholics sufficiently aware of the
reality of Mary and the Saints? Do the example and intercession of Mary and the Saints sustain our people in
responding to the universal vocation to holiness? Do we
understand the Church's liturgy as a participation in the
heavenly liturgy? Would a recovery of that understanding
help to reinvigorate attendance at Sunday Mass?

6. The Church in the United States has been enriched
by a great diversity of expressions of faith found among
people of different ethnic backgrounds. This rich diversity
indicates that the Church is catholic in the full sense, embracing all peoples and cultures. Yet the Church, with all
her different members, remains the one Body of Christ.

Diversity in the Church must serve the unity of the one faith, the one baptism (cf. Eph. 4:5), so that "speaking the truth in love, we grow up in every way into him who is the head, into Christ, from whom the whole body, joined and knit together . . . builds itself up in love" (Eph. 4:15–16). Respect for a specific culture and tradition must always be accompanied by faithfulness to the essential truth of the Gospel as passed down in the teaching of the Church.

A particularly rich form of the diversity which builds up the Body of Christ is found in *the Eastern-rite Churches* present alongside the Latin Church in many parts of your country. I am especially pleased to greet the Archeparchs and Eparchs taking part in this *ad limina* visit. The Eastern Catholics who live in the United States constitute a natural bridge between East and West. On the one hand they make known by direct experience the Christian East and, on the other, they contribute to the development of the Oriental Churches in their countries of origin by witnessing to the acquisitions of the West and by providing spiritual and material support for people in their homeland. In order to fulfill this twofold task, it is essential that they maintain and deepen the sense of belonging to their specific ecclesial tradition, making use of the indications offered in the *Instruction for the Application of the Liturgical Prescriptions of the Code of Canons of the Oriental Churches*, issued by the Congregation for the Oriental Churches.

The Pastors of the Eastern Churches face new and demanding challenges in ensuring that the faithful recently arrived in the United States are properly integrated into their respective ecclesial communities. Serious consideration must also be given to ways of addressing the problems arising from the dispersal of the faithful, who continue to leave the areas where their community was traditionally present and where their ecclesial identity was more easily preserved, to live in other parts of the country.

These aspects highlight the great need for *close collaboration between Latin and Oriental Bishops* in order to safeguard and guarantee the legitimate diversity which constitutes the richness of the Church's universality. I urge my Brother Bishops of the Latin rite to foster greater knowledge and appreciation of the Eastern heritage which is an integral part of the Catholic expression of the faith. In this way all the faithful will have a more thorough understanding of the Christian experience, and the Catholic community will be capable of giving a more complete Christian response to the expectations of the men and women of today (cf. Apostolic Letter *Orientale Lumen*, 5).

7.   Dear Brother Bishops, as we look forward in hope to the celebration of the Great Jubilee of the Year 2000, I pray that the priests, deacons, religious and lay faithful of your Dioceses will be inspired to grow in their love of the Church, and thus come into an ever more profound union with Christ the Bridegroom. The most important aspect of our preparation for the celebration of the two-thousandth anniversary of the Incarnation is our response to the call to that holiness "without which no one shall see the Lord" (Heb. 12:14). For it is only in the grace of the Holy Spirit that God's people can truly challenge society by their untiring and courageous witness to the truth. Entrusting you and all those whom you serve to the maternal care of Mary, I cordially impart my Apostolic Blessing.

— From the Vatican, March 12, 1998

III

Called to the New Evangelization

Dear Cardinal Hickey and Cardinal Keeler,
Dear Brother Bishops,

1. I warmly welcome you, the Pastors of the ecclesiastical provinces of *Baltimore, Washington, Atlanta and Miami*. Your visit *ad limina* is a time of grace as you *pray at the tombs of the Apostles Peter and Paul* who fearlessly proclaimed the Good News of salvation to the point of martyrdom. In entrusting to them your pastoral mission of preaching the "unsearchable riches of Christ" and of making known "the plan of the mystery hidden for ages in God who created all things" (Eph. 3:8–9), may you feel reassured that you are not alone in your task; the Lord provides the strength and the means necessary for you to fulfill his command: "preach the Gospel to the whole creation" (Mark 16:15).

In my meetings with the first two groups of Bishops from your country, we have reflected together on the reception in your country of the great grace of the Second Vatican Council. In those reflections I referred to two essential elements of your episcopal ministry in the cultural context of the United States. First, because the message we preach is God's wisdom, not our own, everything in the life of the Church must correspond to "the truth that has been entrusted to you by the Holy Spirit who dwells within us" (2 Tim. 1:14). Secondly, the purpose of our ministry is to lead the members of the Church into a living communion with God and with one another. That *communio*, according to the Council, is the very heart of the Church's understanding of herself.

In this meeting, I would like to reflect with you on the truth that *the pilgrim Church is missionary by her very nature*, for the universal community of Christ's followers, present in and living through the particular Churches, is the continuation in time of the eternal mission of the Son and of the Holy Spirit (cf. *Ad Gentes*, 2). As the whole Church prepares for the Great Jubilee of the Year 2000, I am confident that you will seek to renew among your communities a vital, dynamic sense of the Church's mission, so that this time of grace may be a new springtime for the Gospel. This is the hope and determination which inspired the recent Special Assembly for America of the Synod of Bishops, which issued a compelling call to conversion, communion and solidarity. This same hope and determination inspires what you have written in your own National Plan and Strategy for Catholic Evangelization in the United States, *Go and Make Disciples*, which is a significant and valid guide in your efforts "to bring about in all Catholics such an enthusiasm for their faith that, in living their faith in Jesus, they freely share it with others" (*loc. cit.*, 1).

2. In that document you rightly insist that "evangelization can only happen when people accept the Gospel freely as the 'good news' it is meant to be, because of the power of the Gospel message and the accompanying grace

of Christ." Evangelization is the Church's effort to proclaim to everyone that God loves them, that he has given himself for them in Christ Jesus, and that he invites them to an unending life of happiness. Once this Gospel has been accepted as the "good news," it demands to be shared. All baptized Christians must commit themselves to evangelization, conscious that God is already at work in the minds and hearts of their listeners, just as he prompted the Ethiopian to ask for baptism when Philip told him "the good news of Jesus" (Acts 8:35). Evangelization is thus a part of the great mystery of God's self-revelation to the world: it involves the human effort to preach the Gospel and the powerful work of the Holy Spirit in those who encounter its saving message. Since we are proclaiming a mystery, we are the servants of a supernatural gift, which surpasses anything our human minds are capable of fully grasping or explaining, yet which attracts by its own inner logic and beauty.

3. *The spirit of the new evangelization should inspire every aspect of your teaching, instruction and catechesis.* These tasks involve a vital effort to come to a deeper understanding of the mysteries of faith and to find meaningful language with which to convince our contemporaries that they are called to newness of life through God's love. Since love can only be understood by someone who actually loves, the Christian mystery can only be effectively communicated by those who allow themselves to be genuinely possessed by God's love. Thus the passing on of the faith, according to the Church's tradition, needs to be carried out in a spiritual environment of friendship with God, rooted in a love which will one day find its fulfilment in the contemplation of God himself. Everyone has a part to play in this

great effort. Your task is to inspire priests, deacons, religious and faithful to have the courage and the conviction to share their faith with others. By proclaiming the Gospel, Christians help others to satisfy the yearning for fullness of life and truth which exists in every human heart.

4. The parish will necessarily be the center of the new evangelization, and thus parish life must be renewed in all its dimensions. During the parish visitations I undertook as Archbishop of Kraków, I always made an effort to stress that the parish is not an accidental collection of Christians who happen to live in the same neighborhood. Rather, because the parish makes present and in a sense incarnates the Mystical Body of Christ, the threefold *munus* ("office") of Christ as prophet, priest, and king must be exercised there. Thus the parish must be a place where, through *worship in communion of doctrine and life with the Bishop and with the Universal Church*, the members of Christ's body are formed for evangelization and works of Christian love. A parish will be involved in many activities. But none is as vital or as community-forming as the Sunday celebration of the Lord's Day and his Eucharist (cf. *Catechism of the Catholic Church*, no. 2177). Through regular and fervent reception of the sacraments, God's people come to know the fullness of the Christian dignity that is theirs by baptism; they are elevated and transformed. Through careful listening to the word of Scripture and sound instruction in the faith they are enabled to experience their lives, and the life of the parish, as a dynamic sharing in the history of salvation. That experience, in turn, becomes a powerful motive for evangelization.

Everything you do to ensure the correct and worthy

celebration of the Eucharist and the other sacraments, precisely because it leads the faithful to a deep and transforming encounter with God, builds up the Church in her inner life and as the visible sign of salvation for the world. Preaching and catechesis should emphasize that the grace of the sacraments is what enables us to live in accordance with the demands of the Gospel. Adoration of the Eucharist outside of the Mass permits a deeper appreciation of the gift that Christ makes to us in his Body and Blood in the Holy Sacrifice of the Altar. Encouragement of frequent recourse to the Sacrament of Penance increases the spiritual maturity of all parishioners as they strive to commit themselves to witnessing to the truth of the Gospel in private and public life.

5. The strength of parish life in your country can be judged above all from the way families pass on the faith to each succeeding generation, and from the impressive and essential system of Catholic schools that you and your predecessors have built and sustained at great sacrifice. As a priest and Bishop I have always been convinced that ministry to families is an extremely important dimension of the Church's evangelizing task since "the family itself is the first and most appropriate place for teaching the truths of the faith, the practice of Christian virtues and the essential values of human life" (*Address at Our Lady of Guadalupe Plaza*, San Antonio, September 13, 1987, no. 4). Catholic schools for their part must have a specific Catholic identity, and those who administer them and teach in them have a responsibility to uphold and communicate the truths, values and ideals which constitute a truly Catholic education. Many of your parishes have committed themselves to

winning inactive Catholics back to the practice of the faith and to reaching out to all those in search of the truth of the Gospel. These efforts are a profound expression of the essential missionary nature of the Church which should mark every parish community. I am aware of the complexities of parish life in the United States and of the burden of work borne by priests, deacons, religious, and laity as they face the daily challenge of inspiring God's people to live the Gospel more fully and build a society imbued with Christian values. Be close to all those who work in parishes, sustaining them with your prayer and wise counsel, endeavoring to create in everyone the *sensus Ecclesiae*, a vivid sense of what belonging to the Church means in practical terms.

6. At the recent Special Session for America of the Synod of Bishops, the Bishops called on all the faithful to be "evangelists of the new millennium," by witnessing to the faith through lives of holiness, kindness to all, charity to those in need and solidarity with all the oppressed (cf. *Message to America*, no. 30). In living the faith and communicating it to others in a culture that tends to treat religious convictions as merely a personal "option," evangelization's only point of departure is Jesus Christ, "the Way, and the Truth and the Life" (John 14:6), the answer to the question that is every human life. As you lead the Church in the United States in preparation for the Great Jubilee, help everyone in the Catholic community to understand that we know, love, worship, and serve God, not as a response to some psychological "need," but as a duty whose fulfillment is an expression of man's highest dignity and the source of man's most profound happiness. An essential part of your ministry must be to help all sectors of the Catholic com-

munity find greater certainty about what the Church actually teaches, and greater serenity in confronting the many issues which — often needlessly — cause division and polarization among those who should be of one mind and heart (cf. Acts 2:44). As the recent Synod said, all must be encouraged "to turn from hesitant and wary steps, to walk in joy with Jesus on the road to everlasting life" (*Message to America*, no. 37).

Because Christians have come to know Christ and the liberating force of his Gospel, they have *a particular responsibility to contribute to the renewal of culture.* In this task, which pertains in a special way to the laity, Christ's followers should not cease to make present in all areas of public life the light which Christ's teaching sheds on the human condition. In contemporary culture there is often a weakening of the sense of the innate dependence of all human existence on the Creator, the capacity of the human mind to know the truth, and the validity of the universal and unchanging moral norms which guide all people in the fulfillment of their human vocation. When freedom is detached from the truth about the human person and from the moral law inscribed in human nature, then society and its democratic form of life are imperiled. For if freedom is not linked to truth and ordered to goodness, "the ground is laid for society to be at the mercy of the unrestrained will of individuals or the oppressive totalitarianism of public authority" (*Evangelium Vitae*, 96). In proclaiming the truths about the human person, human community and human destiny that they know from revelation and reason, Christians make an indispensable contribution to sustaining a free society, a society in which freedom nurtures genuine human development.

7. Dear Brother Bishops, as we approach the next Christian Millennium, encourage all Catholics in the United States to deepen their commitment to the Church's evangelizing mission. Lead them by your example, your conviction and your teaching. I pray that the Holy Spirit will enlighten you and help you to inspire your people, so that the hearts of the faithful will burn more brightly with love for Christ and a desire to make him better known. Entrusting you and all the priests, religious and laity of your Dioceses to Mary, Mother of the Redeemer, I cordially impart my Apostolic Blessing.

— From the Vatican, March 17, 1998

IV

Pastoral Ministry of Bishops

Dear Brother Bishops,

1. Following the visits of other groups of Bishops of the United States, I now warmly welcome you, *the Bishops of the ecclesiastical provinces of Louisville, Mobile and New Orleans*. Through you I greet each member of the Dioceses in which the Holy Spirit has made you overseers to care for the Church of God (cf. Acts 20:28). In a special way I thank God for the bonds of communion which unite us in the episcopal ministry at the service of his holy people. The Church's experience since the Second Vatican Council illustrates how important the ministry of the Bishop is for the renewal which the Council advocated and for the new evangelization which must be undertaken on the threshold of the Third Christian Millennium. And so I propose to reflect today on some of the more fundamental aspects of this ministry of ours, which comes to us from the Apostles "in a sequence running back to the beginning" (*Lumen Gentium*, 20).

2. In your document *The Teaching Ministry of the Diocesan Bishop*, you drew attention to an important truth: *the episcopal ministry is a crucial part of God's saving work in human history*. It cannot be reduced to "a variation of the

common human need for organization and authority" (*loc. cit.*, 1, A, 1). It is in fact by the mandate and command of Christ that Bishops teach "the unchanging faith of the Church as it is to be understood and lived today" (*ibid.*, 1, A, 2). This duty can only be understood and fulfilled in the context of *a Bishop's personal adherence to the faith*. In fact, the Lord's mandate to his Apostles to teach in his name is not without a connection to a profound act of faith on their part: the act of faith by which the apostles, with Peter, recognized that Jesus was "the Christ, the Son of the living God" (Matt. 16:16). That same profession of faith in Christ must always be at the heart of a Bishop's life and ministry.

In his Diocese the Bishop declares the faith of the Church with *the authority which derives from his episcopal ordination and from communion with the College of Bishops under its Head* (cf. *Lumen Gentium*, 22). His task is to teach in a pastoral way, illuminating modern problems with the light of the Gospel and helping the faithful to live full Christian lives amid the challenges of our times (cf. *Directory on the Pastoral Ministry of Bishops*, 56). In applying the Gospel to new issues while safeguarding the authentic interpretation of the Church's teaching, the Bishop ensures that the local Church abides in the truth which saves and liberates. All this requires that the Bishop be a man of firm supernatural faith and steadfast loyalty to Christ and his Church.

3. Our teaching carries with it a great responsibility since it is "endowed with the authority of Christ" (*Lumen Gentium*, 25); yet we must teach and preach with great humility since we are the servants of the word, not its masters.

If we are to be effective teachers, we must allow our entire existence to be transformed by prayer and the continuous submission of ourselves to God in imitation of Christ himself. To satisfy the thirst among the People of God for the truth of the Gospel, we Bishops should take heed of Saint Charles Borromeo's words to his priests at his last Synod: "Is your duty preaching and teaching? Concentrate carefully on what is essential to fulfil that office fittingly. Make sure in the first place that your life and conduct are sermons in themselves" (*Liturgy of the Hours*, Feast of Saint Charles).

Preaching the Gospel message effectively requires constant personal prayer, study, reflection, and consultation with knowledgeable advisers. Commitment to the study and scholarship demanded by the *munus episcopale* is crucial in guarding "the truth that has been entrusted to us by the Holy Spirit who dwells within us" (cf. 2 Tim. 1:14) and in proclaiming it with power "in and out of season" (*ibid.*, 4:2). Since the Bishop has a *personal responsibility* to teach the faith, he needs time to assimilate the content of the Church's tradition and Magisterium prayerfully. Likewise, he should be familiar with helpful developments in theology, in biblical studies and in moral reflection on social issues. I know from my own experience as a diocesan Bishop the many demands that are made on a Bishop's time. Yet that experience convinced me that it is essential to make time, intentionally, for study and reflection. For it is only through study and reflection and prayer that the Bishop, working with his collaborators, can guide and govern in a truly Christian and ecclesial manner, always asking himself: "What is the truth of faith that sheds light on the problem we are addressing?" Thus the Bishop today may need to re-organize the way in which he exercises his episcopal office in order to attend to what is fundamental in his ministry.

4. The Great Jubilee of the Year 2000 calls us to redouble our efforts to preach the Gospel in response to the deep-rooted desire for spiritual truth that characterizes our times. This "hour" of evangelization makes special demands on Bishops. In *The Teaching Ministry of the Diocesan Bishop*, you identified the qualities which render a Bishop's teaching effective. Through his pastoral experience, study, reflection, judgment and prayer, he must *make the salvific truth his own* so that he can communicate the fullness of faith and encourage the faithful in living according to the demands of the Gospel. The Bishop is charged with transmitting the faith he has received; hence he must see his teaching as a humble service to the word of God and the Church's tradition. Being ready to suffer for the sake of the Gospel (cf. 2 Tim. 1:8), he must proclaim the truth courageously, even if this means challenging socially acceptable opinion. The Bishop should teach frequently and constantly, preaching homilies, writing pastoral letters, giving conferences and making use of the media, in such a way that *he is seen to teach the faith and so bear public witness to the Gospel*. Moreover, his teaching should be marked by charity, in accordance with Paul's words to Timothy: "the Lord's servant must not be quarrelsome but kindly to every one, an apt teacher, forbearing, correcting his opponents with gentleness" (2 Tim. 2:24–25).

5. "Tend the flock of God that is your charge" (1 Pet. 5:2). Any reflection on your responsibility for *the pastoral*

governance of that part of God's People entrusted to you "as the vicars and ambassadors of Christ" (*Lumen Gentium*, 27) must begin from careful consideration of the example of Christ himself, the Good Shepherd, our supreme model. In the recent Special Assembly for America of the Synod of Bishops, many Pastors raised questions about the example of their own lives and ministry, knowing that *the People of God will heed their voice and respond if their witness is perceived as authentic*. In the Synod Hall we heard the call for Bishops as individuals and as a body to become more simple, with the simplicity of Jesus and of the Gospel — a simplicity which consists in being immersed in the essential things of the Father (cf. Luke 2:49).

In order to meet the needs of modern times, Dioceses have frequently developed complex structures and a variety of diocesan offices which provide assistance in the exercise of pastoral government. As Bishops, however, you must be careful to safeguard *the personal nature of your governance*, devoting much time to knowing the strengths and weaknesses of your Dioceses, the faithful's expectations and needs, their traditions and charisms, the social context in which they live, and the long-term problems which need to be addressed. This means ensuring that the structures necessary today in leading a diocese do not impede the very thing they are meant to facilitate: *a Bishop's contact with his people and his role as an evangelist*. In the Synod it was pointed out that it is all too easy today for a Bishop to yield his evangelizing and catechizing responsibility to others and become a captive of his own administrative obligations. Since our ministry is always directed to *the building up of the body of the Church in truth and holiness* (cf. *Lumen Gentium*, 27), the exercise of episcopal authority is never a mere administrative necessity but a *witness* to the truth about God and man revealed in Jesus Christ and a *service* for the good of all. In order to lead people to the fullness of Jesus Christ we must in fact "do the work of the evangelist" (2 Tim. 4:5). No other task is as urgent as this.

6. In a special way a diocesan Bishop must make every effort to maintain a close relationship with his priests, a relationship characterized by charity and concern for their spiritual and material well-being. In promoting an atmosphere of mutual confidence and trust, he is to be a teacher, father, friend and brother to them (cf. *Directory for the Pastoral Ministry of Bishops*, 107). In this way the juridical bond of obedience between priest and Bishop is animated by that supernatural charity which existed between Christ and his disciples. This pastoral charity and spirit of communion between Bishop and priests is vital for the effectiveness of the apostolate. Likewise, *it must be the Bishop's special care to reach out to young men whom Christ is calling to share in his priesthood* through the ordained ministry. Experience has shown that when the local Bishop takes this responsibility seriously, there is no "vocation shortage." Young men want to be called to radical self-giving, and the Bishop, insofar as he is the one principally responsible for the continuation of Christ's saving mission in the world, is the one who can repeat Christ's words with authority: "Follow me, and I will make you fishers of men" (Matt. 4:19).

The relation between the Bishop and members of religious communities should likewise be inspired by his *esteem for the consecrated life and his commitment to making the various charisms known in the local Church*, again with an eye to inviting young people to live out their baptismal grace by generously embracing the evangelical counsels. Moreover, since the Council we are all more aware of the need to *recognize, safeguard and promote the dignity, rights and duties of the lay faithful.* It is essential that their service to the ecclesial community, their counsel, and their efforts to bring the Church's teaching to bear on contemporary culture through the transformation of intellectual, political and economic life be appreciated and encouraged by the Bishop and his close collaborators.

7. The aftermath of the Second Vatican Council witnessed the development of *Episcopal Conferences as instruments for exercising that collegiality among Bishops which springs from ordination and hierarchical communion.* The Conference exists to foster the sharing of pastoral experience and to allow for a common approach to various questions that arise in the life of the Church in a particular region or country. Your recent decision to study the structure and functions of your Conference suggests that you recognize a need to rethink its operations so that they may better serve the pastoral and evangelical purposes that give the Conference its unique meaning.

Among other things, this means that the Episcopal Conference must find a way to be truly effective without weakening the teaching and pastoral authority which belongs to Bishops alone. Its administrative structures must not become ends in themselves but always remain instruments of the great tasks of evangelization and ecclesial service. Special care must be taken to ensure that the Conference functions as *an ecclesial body* and not as an institution reflecting the management models of secular society. In this

way each Bishop will be enabled to bring his unique gifts
to bear on the discussions and decisions of the Conference.
The Bishop's duty to teach, sanctify and govern is in fact a
personal one which cannot be surrendered to others.

8. We can never remind ourselves too often that the
Pastors of the Church are personally *responsible for passing*
on the light and joy of the faith. To say this is immediately to
confront *the question of our own faith and conviction.* Your *ad*
limina visit, with your prayer at the tombs of the Apostles
Peter and Paul, offers a grace-filled occasion to remember
how essential to your witness is *your own relationship to*
Christ and the seriousness of your personal quest for holiness.
The vitality of your local Churches and the well-being of
the universal Church is first and always a gift of the Holy
Spirit. But that gift is not independent of the ardent prayer
and self-giving pastoral charity of the Bishops, as individuals and as a body. In our weaknesses we need to be sustained by the grace of the Holy Spirit in order to be able to
say without fear: "Lord, to whom shall we go? You have
the words of eternal life; *and we have believed, and have*
come to know, that you are the Holy One of God" (John 6:68,
69). On the two-thousandth anniversary of the Incarnation,
may the Church — the Bride — offer her Lord an episcopal college united and steadfast in faith, ardent in bearing
witness to the Gospel of God's grace, and dedicated to the
ministration of the Spirit and of God's glorious power to
make men just (cf. *Lumen Gentium*, 21).

Dear Brothers, with these reflections on your ministry,
I wish to encourage you in the grace and vocation that
Christ has bestowed upon you. I pray for you as you go
about your task of proclaiming the love of God and the

mysteries of salvation to all, confident that the Holy Spirit will guide and fortify you. In gratitude for your work in preaching the word of God "with unfailing patience and sound teaching" (2 Tim. 4:2), I commend you to the intercession of the Blessed Virgin Mary, *Sedes Sapientiae*, that she may sustain you in pastoral wisdom and bring joy and peace to your hearts. To you and the priests, religious and lay faithful of your Dioceses, I cordially impart my Apostolic Blessing.

— From the Vatican, March 30, 1998

V

Gift of the Priesthood

Dear Cardinal Maida,
Dear Brother Bishops,

1. On the occasion of your *ad limina* visit, I welcome with great joy the fifth group of *Bishops from the United States, from the States of Michigan and Ohio*. Your pilgrimage to the tombs of the Apostles Peter and Paul provides a fresh opportunity to reflect on the witness which they gave *usque ad sanguinis effusionem*, and expresses the profound bond of communion which exists between the Bishops and the Successor of Peter. These days are therefore a time of reflection on your own ministry as Bishops and your special responsibility before Christ for the well-being of his body, the Church. May the example of the first witnesses and their intercession be a source of strength to you in preaching the Gospel, bearing in mind Saint Paul's words to Timothy: "the aim of our charge is love that issues from a pure heart and a good conscience and sincere faith" (1 Tim. 1:5).

In this series of *ad limina* talks, I have chosen to reflect on the opportunities presented by the Great Jubilee of the Year 2000 for *evangelization in the light of the extraordinary grace which was and is the Second Vatican Council*. At my last meeting with Bishops from your country, I referred to the distinctive apostolic character of the Bishop's own ministry and its importance for the spiritual renewal of the Christian community. Today I wish to mention the identity and mission of *priests, your co-workers in the task of sanctifying the people of God and handing on the faith* (cf. *Lumen Gentium*, 28). With immense gratitude I think of all your priests whose lives are deeply marked by fidelity to Christ and generous dedication to their brothers and sisters.

2. Two years ago I celebrated my own Fiftieth Anniversary of ordination, and I can truly say that my experience of the priesthood has been a source of great joy to me throughout these years. Reflecting on the priesthood in *Gift and Mystery*, I emphasized two essential truths. The priestly vocation is a *mystery* of divine election, and therefore a *gift* which infinitely transcends the individual. As I look back, I am constantly reminded of the words of Jesus to his Apostles: "You did not choose me, but I chose you and appointed you that you should go and bear fruit and that your fruit should abide" (John 15:16). In meditating on these words, a priest becomes more aware of *the mysterious choice that God has made* in calling him to this service, not because of his talents or merits but in virtue of God's "own purpose and the grace which he gave us" (2 Tim. 1:9).

It is vital for the life of the Church in your Dioceses that you devote much attention to your priests and to the *quality* of their life and ministry. Through word and example you should constantly remind them that the priesthood is a special vocation which consists in being uniquely *configured to Christ the High Priest, the teacher, sanctifier and shepherd of his people*, through the imposition of hands and the invocation of the Holy Spirit in the Sacrament of Holy Orders. It is not a career, nor does it mean belonging to a

clerical caste. For this reason "the priest must be conscious
that his life is a mystery totally grafted on to the mystery of
Christ and of the Church in a new and specific way and this
engages him totally in pastoral activity" (*Directory on the
Ministry and Life of Priests*, no. 6). Thus the priest's whole
life is transformed so that he may *be Christ* for others: a
convincing and efficacious sign of God's loving and saving
presence. He should live the priesthood as *a total gift of
himself to the Lord*. And if this gift is to be authentic, his
thoughts, attitudes, activity and relations with others must
all show that he has truly put on the "mind of Christ"
(cf. 1 Cor. 2:16). With Saint Paul he should be able to say:
"It is no longer I who live, but Christ who lives in me;
and the life I now live in the flesh I live by faith in the
Son of God, who loved me and gave himself for me" (Gal.
2:20). We should gratefully recognize the signs of a genuine
renewal of the spirituality of the priesthood, and foster a
fresh blossoming of the authentic theological tradition of
priestly life wherever it may have become obscured.

3.   If Bishops and priests are to be truly effective witnesses to Christ and teachers of the faith, they have to
be *men of prayer like Christ himself*. Only by turning frequently and trustingly to God and seeking the guidance
of the Holy Spirit can a priest fulfill his mission. Priests,
and seminarians preparing for the priesthood, need to in-
teriorize the fact that there is "an intimate bond between
the priest's spiritual life and the exercise of his ministry"
(*Pastores Dabo Vobis*, 24). Every priest is called to develop a
great personal familiarity with the word of God, so that he
may enter ever more completely into the Master's thought
and strengthen his attachment to the Lord, his priestly

model and guide (cf. *General Audience*, June 2, 1993, no. 4). A committed prayer-life brings the gift of wisdom, with which "the Spirit leads the priest to evaluate all things in the light of the Gospel, helping him to read in his own experience and the experience of the Church the mysterious and loving plan of the Father" (*Letter to Priests 1998,* no. 5).

At a time when many demands are made on the priest's time and energies, it is important to emphasize that *one of his first duties is to pray on behalf of the people entrusted to him.* This is his privilege and his responsibility, for he has been ordained to represent his people before the Lord and to intercede on their behalf before the throne of grace (cf. *General Audience*, June 2, 1993, no. 5). In this regard, I would emphasize again the importance in priestly life of faithfully praying the *Liturgy of the Hours, the public prayer of the Church*, every day. While the faithful are invited to participate in this prayer, following Christ's recommendation to pray at all times without losing heart (cf. Luke 18:1), priests have received a special commission to celebrate the Divine Office, in which Christ himself prays with us and for us (cf. *Letter to Priests 1984*, no. 5). Indeed prayer for the needs of the Church and the individual faithful is so important that serious thought should be given to reorganizing priestly and parish life to ensure that priests have time to devote to this essential task, individually and in common. Liturgical and personal prayer, not the tasks of management, must define the rhythms of a priest's life, even in the busiest of parishes.

4. The celebration of the Eucharist is the most important moment of the priest's day, the center of his life.

Offering the Sacrifice of the Mass, in which the unique sacrifice of Christ is made present and applied until he comes again, the priest ensures that the work of redemption continues to be carried out (cf. *Presbyterorum Ordinis*, 13). From this unique Sacrifice, the priest's entire ministry draws its strength (cf. *ibid.*, 2) and the People of God receive the grace to live truly Christian lives in the family and in society. It is important for Bishops and priests not to lose sight of the *intrinsic value of the Eucharist*, a value which is independent of the circumstances surrounding its celebration. For this reason, priests should be encouraged to celebrate Mass every day, even in the absence of a congregation, since it is an act of Christ and the Church (cf. *ibid.*, 13; *Code of Canon Law*, c. 904).

In order that the Eucharist may fully produce its grace in the life of your communities, specific attention also needs to be given to promoting the Sacrament of Penance. *Priests are the special witnesses and ministers of God's mercy.* At no other time can they be as close to the faithful as when they lead them to the crucified and forgiving Christ in this uniquely personal encounter (cf. *Redemptor Hominis*, 20). To be the minister of the Sacrament of Reconciliation is a special privilege for a priest who, acting in the person of Christ, is permitted to enter into the drama of another Christian life in a singular way. Priests should always be available to hear the confessions of the faithful, and to do so in a way that allows the penitent's particular situation to unfold and be reflected upon in the light of the Gospel. This fundamental task of the pastoral ministry, directed to intensifying the union of each individual with the Father of mercies, is a vital dimension of the Church's mission. It should be the subject of study and reflection in priests' gatherings and in courses of continuing formation. To cut oneself off from the Sacrament of Penance is to cut oneself off from an irreplaceable form of encounter with Christ. So, priests themselves should receive this sacrament regularly and in a spirit of genuine faith and devotion. In this way, the priest's own constant conversion to the Lord is strengthened, and the faithful see more clearly that reconciliation with God and the Church is necessary for authentic Christian living (cf. *Directory on the Ministry and Life of Priests*, 53).

5. As teachers of the faith, priests play a direct role in responding to the great challenge of evangelization facing the Church as we prepare to enter the third Christian millennium. *The Gospel we preach is the truth about God and about man and the human condition*: the people of our time want to hear this truth in all its fullness. Thus the Sunday homily requires careful preparation on the part of the priest, who is personally responsible for helping the faithful to see how the Gospel sheds light on the path of individuals and of society (cf. *General Audience*, April 21, 1993, no. 5). The *Catechism of the Catholic Church* is an excellent resource for preaching, and by using it priests will help their communities to grow in knowledge of the Christian mystery in all its inexhaustible richness, and so help them to be grounded in true holiness and strengthened for witness and service (cf. *Letter to Priests for Holy Thursday*, 8 April 1993, no. 2).

The parish is a "family of families" and should be organized to support family life in every way possible. My own experience as a young priest in Krakow taught me how much *the assistance that priests can give to young couples as they prepare for the responsibilities of married life is also of great benefit to their own priestly spirituality.* Priests are called to a unique form of spiritual fatherhood and can come to a deeper appreciation of the meaning of being a "man for others" through their pastoral care of those striving to live out the requirements of self-giving and fruitful love in Christian marriage.

It is the priest's task to lead the faithful to spiritual maturity in Christ, so that they may respond to the call to holiness and fulfill their vocation to transform the world in the spirit of the Gospel (cf. *Christifideles Laici*, 36). In collaborating closely with the laity, priests must encourage them to see the Gospel as the principal force for the renewal of society — the vast and complex world of politics and economics, but also the world of culture, of the sciences and the arts, of international life, of the mass media (cf. *Evangelii Nuntiandi*, 70). A priest need not be an expert in all these things, but he should be an expert in discerning the "higher gifts" which the Holy Spirit abundantly pours out for the building of the Kingdom (cf. 1 Cor. 12:31), and he should help his people apply those gifts in advancing a civilization of love.

6. A Bishop cannot fail to be personally involved in the promotion of vocations to the priesthood, and he needs to encourage the whole community of faith to play an active role in this work. "The time has come to speak courageously about priestly life as a priceless gift and a splendid and privileged form of Christian living" (*Pastores Dabo Vobis*, 39). Experience shows that when the invitation is made, the response is generous. A priest's pastoral contact with young people, his closeness to them in their problems, his

attitude of openness, benevolence and availability, are all part of authentic youth ministry. A priest is a true spiritual guide when *he helps young people to make important decisions about their lives*, and especially when he helps them to answer the question: what does Christ want of me? More needs to be done to ensure that all priests are convinced of the fundamental importance of this aspect of the ministry. In the promotion and discernment of priestly vocations, there is no substitute for the presence of a committed, mature and happy priest with whom young people can meet and talk.

7. As Bishops, you must explain to the faithful why the Church does not have authority to ordain women to the ministerial priesthood, at the same time making clear why this is not a question of the equality of persons or of their God-given rights. The Sacrament of Holy Orders and the ministerial priesthood are given by God as a gift: in the first place, to the Church; and then to the individual called by God. Thus ordination to the ministerial priesthood can never be claimed by anyone as a right; no one is "due" Holy Orders within the economy of salvation. That discernment belongs, finally, to the Church, through the Bishop. And the Church ordains only on the basis of that ecclesial and episcopal discernment.

The Church's teaching that only men may be ordained to the ministerial priesthood is an expression of fidelity to the witness of the New Testament and the constant tradition of the Church of East and West. The fact that Jesus himself chose and commissioned men for certain specific tasks did not in any way diminish the human dignity of women (which he clearly intended to emphasize and defend); nor by doing so did he relegate women to a merely passive role in the Christian community. The New Testament makes it clear that women played a vital part in the early Church. The New Testament witness and the constant tradition of the Church remind us that the ministerial priesthood cannot be understood in sociological or political categories, as a matter of exercising "power" within the community. The priesthood of Holy Orders must be understood theologically, as one form of service in and for the Church. There are many forms of such service, as there are many gifts given by the same Spirit (1 Cor. 12:4–11).

The Churches — in particular the Catholic and Orthodox Churches — which set sacramentality at the heart of the Christian life, and the Eucharist at the heart of sacramentality, are those which claim no authority to ordain women to the ministerial priesthood. Conversely, Christian communities more readily confer a ministerial responsibility on women the further they move away from a sacramental understanding of the Church, the Eucharist, and the priesthood. This is a phenomenon that needs to be explored more deeply by theologians in collaboration with the Bishops. At the same time, it is indispensable that you continue to pay attention to the whole question of how women's specific gifts are nurtured, accepted, and brought to fruition in the ecclesial community (cf. *Letter to Women*, 11–12). The "genius" of women must be ever more a vital strength of the Church of the next millennium, just as it was in the first communities of Christ's disciples.

8.   Dear Brother Bishops, through you I would like to reach out to all the priests of the United States, to thank them for the holiness of their lives and for their untiring

zeal in helping the faithful to experience God's saving love. The joyful and responsible witness of your priests is an extraordinary tribute to the vitality of the Church in your Dioceses. I invite you and them to renew each day your love for the priesthood and always to see in it the pearl of great price for which a man will sacrifice all else (cf. Matt. 13:45). I pray especially for those who are experiencing difficulties in their vocation, and I entrust their worries and cares to the intercession of Mary, Mother of the Redeemer.

As we celebrate today the Feast of the Ascension, we rejoice in the Lord's glory at the right hand of the Father and we look towards the approaching Feast of Pentecost. I invoke a fresh outpouring of the Holy Spirit upon you and upon the priests, Religious and laity of your Dioceses. May the Paraclete who guides the Church in the task of evangelization renew his sevenfold gift in your hearts, so that with total fidelity you may love and serve the particular Churches entrusted to your care. With my Apostolic Blessing.

— From the Vatican, May 21, 1998

VI

The Church's
Educational Mission

Dear Cardinal George,
Dear Brother Bishops,

1. In the course of this series of *ad limina* visits, the
Bishops of the United States have again borne witness to
the keen sense of communion of American Catholics with
the Successor of Peter. From the beginning of my Pontificate I have experienced this closeness, and the spiritual and
material support of so many of your people. In welcoming
you, *the Bishops of the ecclesiastical regions of Chicago, Indi-
anapolis and Milwaukee*, I express once more to you and to
the whole Church in your country my heartfelt gratitude:
"God is my witness, whom I serve with my spirit in the
Gospel of his Son, that without ceasing I mention you always in my prayers" (Rom. 1:9). Continuing the reflection
begun with previous groups of Bishops on *the renewal of
ecclesial life in the light of the Second Vatican Council and in
view of the challenge of evangelization which we face on the
eve of the next millennium*, today I wish to address some
aspects of your responsibility for Catholic education.

2. From the earliest days of the American Republic,
when Archbishop John Carroll encouraged the teaching

vocation of Saint Elizabeth Ann Seton and founded the new nation's first Catholic college, *the Church in the United States has been deeply involved in education at every level.* For more than two hundred years, Catholic elementary schools, high schools, colleges and universities have been instrumental in educating successive generations of Catholics, and in teaching the *truths* of the faith, promoting respect for the human person, and developing the moral character of their students. Their academic excellence and success in preparing young people for life have served the whole of American society.

As we approach the third Christian millennium, the Second Vatican Council's call for generous dedication to the whole enterprise of Catholic education remains to be more fully implemented (cf. *Gravissimum Educationis*, 1). Few areas of Catholic life in the United States need the leadership of the Bishops for their re-affirmation and renewal as much as this one does. Any such renewal requires *a clear vision of the Church's educational mission*, which in turn cannot be separated from the Lord's mandate *to preach the Gospel* to all nations. Like other educational institutions, Catholic schools transmit knowledge and promote the human development of their students. However, as the Council emphasized, the Catholic school does something else: "It aims to create for the school community an atmosphere enlivened by the Gospel spirit of freedom and charity. It aims to help the young person in such a way that the development of his or her own personality will be matched by the growth of that new creation which he or she has become by baptism. It strives to relate all human culture eventually to the news of salvation, so that the light of faith will illumine the knowledge which students gradually gain of the world, of life, and of the human family" (*ibid.*, 8). *The mission of the Catholic school is the integral formation of students*, so that they may be *true to their condition as Christ's disciples and as such work effectively for the evangelization of culture and for the common good of society*.

3. Catholic education aims not only to communicate facts but also to transmit a coherent, comprehensive vision of life, in the conviction that the truths contained in that vision liberate students in the most profound meaning of human freedom. In its recent document *The Catholic School on the Threshold of the Third Millennium*, the Congregation for Catholic Education drew attention to the importance of communicating knowledge in the context of the Christian vision of the world, of life, of culture and of history: "In the Catholic school there is no separation between time for learning and time for formation, between acquiring notions and growing in wisdom. The various school subjects do not present only knowledge to be attained but also values to be acquired and truths to be discovered" (no. 14).

The greatest challenge to Catholic education in the United States today, and the greatest contribution that authentically Catholic education can make to American culture, is to *restore to that culture the conviction that human beings can grasp the truth of things, and in grasping that truth can know their duties to God, to themselves and their neighbors*. In meeting that challenge, the Catholic educator will hear an echo of Christ's words: "If you continue in my word, you are truly my disciples, and *you will know the truth, and the truth will make you free*" (John 8:32). The contemporary world urgently needs the service of educational institutions which uphold and teach that *truth is "that fundamental value without which freedom, justice and human dignity are extinguished"* (*Veritatis Splendor*, no. 4).

To educate *in the truth*, and *for genuine freedom and evangelical love*, is at the very heart of the Church's mission. In a cultural climate in which moral norms are often thought to be matters of personal preference, Catholic schools have a crucial role to play in leading the younger generation to realize that freedom consists above all in being able to respond to the demands of the truth (cf. *Veritatis Splendor*, no. 84). The respect which Catholic elementary and secondary schools enjoy suggests that their commitment to transmitting moral wisdom is meeting a widely-felt cultural need in your country. The example of Bishops and pastors who, with the support of Catholic parents, have persevered in leadership in this field should encourage everyone's efforts to foster new dedication and new growth. The fact that some Dioceses are involved in a program of school building is a significant sign of vitality and a great hope for the future.

4. Almost twenty-five years have passed since your Conference issued *To Teach as Jesus Did*, a document which is still very relevant today. It emphasized the importance of another aspect of Catholic education: "More than any other program of education sponsored by the Church, the Catholic school has the opportunity and obligation to be . . . oriented to Christian service because it helps students acquire skills, virtues and habits of heart and mind required for effective service to others" (no. 106). On the basis of what they see and hear, students should become ever more aware of the dignity of every human person and gradually absorb the key elements of the Church's social doctrine

and her concern for the poor. Catholic institutions should continue their tradition of *commitment to the education of the poor* in spite of the financial burdens involved. In some cases it may be necessary to find ways to share the burden more evenly, so that parishes with schools are not left to shoulder it alone.

A Catholic school is a place where students live a shared experience of faith in God and where they learn the riches of Catholic culture. Taking proper account of the stages of human development, the freedom of individuals, and the rights of parents in the education of their children, Catholic schools must help students *to deepen their personal relationship with God* and to discover that *all things human have their deepest meaning in the person and teaching of Jesus Christ*. Prayer and the liturgy, especially the Sacraments of the Eucharist and Penance, should mark the rhythm of a Catholic school's life. Transmitting knowledge *about* the faith, though essential, is not sufficient. If students in Catholic schools are to gain a genuine experience of the Church, the example of teachers and others responsible for their formation is crucial: *the witness of adults in the school community is a vital part of the school's identity*.

Numberless religious and lay teachers and other personnel in Catholic schools down the years have shown how their professional competence and commitment are grounded in the spiritual, intellectual and moral values of the Catholic tradition. The Catholic community in the United States and the whole country have been immeasurably blessed through the work of so many dedicated religious in schools in every part of your country. I also know how much you value the dedication of the many lay men and women who, sometimes at great financial sacrifice, are involved in Catholic education because they believe in the mission of Catholic schools. If in some cases there has been an eroding of confidence in the teaching vocation, you must do all you can to restore that trust.

5. *Catechesis*, either in schools or in parish-based programs, plays a fundamental role in transmitting the faith. The Bishop should encourage catechists to see their work as a vocation: as a privileged sharing in the mission of handing on the faith and accounting for the hope that is in us (cf. 1 Pet. 3:15). The Gospel message is the definitive response to the deepest longings of the human heart. *Young Catholics have a right to hear the full content of that message* in order to come to know Christ, the One who has overcome death and opened the way to salvation. Efforts to renew catechesis must be based on the premise that Christ's teaching, as transmitted in the Church and as authentically interpreted by the Magisterium, has to be presented in all its richness, and the methodologies used have to respond to the nature of the faith as truth received (cf. 1 Cor. 15:1). The work you have begun through your Conference to evaluate catechetical texts by the standard of the *Catechism of the Catholic Church* will help to ensure the unity and completeness of the faith as it is presented in your Dioceses.

6. The Church's tradition of involvement in *universities*, which goes back almost a thousand years, quickly took root in the United States. Today Catholic colleges and universities can make an important contribution to the renewal of American higher education. To belong to a university community, as was my privilege during my days as

a professor, is to stand at the crossroads of the cultures that have formed the modern world. It is to be a trustee of the wisdom of centuries and a promoter of the creativity that will transmit that wisdom to future generations. At a time when knowledge is often thought to be fragmentary and never absolute, Catholic universities should be expected to *uphold the objectivity and coherence of knowledge*. Now that the centuries-old conflict between science and faith is fading, Catholic universities should be in the forefront of a new and long-overdue dialogue between the empirical sciences and the truths of faith.

If Catholic universities are to become leaders in the renewal of higher education, they must first have a strong sense of their own Catholic identity. This identity is not established once and for all by an institution's origins, but comes from its living within the Church today and always, speaking from the heart of the Church (*ex corde Ecclesiae*) to the contemporary world. The Catholic identity of a university should be evident in its curriculum, in its faculty, in student activities, and in the quality of its community life. This is no infringement upon the university's nature as a true center of learning, where the truth of the created order is fully respected, but also ultimately illuminated by the light of the new creation in Christ.

The Catholic identity of a university necessarily includes *the university's relationship to the local Church and its Bishop*. It is sometimes said that a university that acknowledges a responsibility to any community or authority outside the relevant academic professional associations has lost both its independence and its integrity. But this is to detach freedom from its object, which is truth. Catholic universities understand that there is no contradiction between the free and vigorous pursuit of the truth and a "recognition of and an adherence to the teaching authority of the Church in matters of faith and morals" (*Ex Corde Ecclesiae*, no. 27).

7. In safeguarding the Catholic identity of Catholic institutions of higher education, Bishops have a special responsibility in relation to the work of theologians. If, as the whole Catholic tradition testifies, *theology is to be done in and for the Church*, then the question of theology's relationship to the teaching authority of the Church is not extrinsic — something imposed from outside — but rather intrinsic to theology as an ecclesial science. Theology itself is accountable to those to whom Christ has given responsibility for overseeing the ecclesial community and its stability in the truth. As the discussion on these questions deepens in your country, it must be the Bishops' aim to see that the terms used are genuinely ecclesial in character.

In addition, *Bishops should take a personal interest in the work of university chaplaincies*, not only in Catholic institutions but also in other colleges and universities where Catholic students are present. Campus ministry offers a notable opportunity to be close to young people at a significant time in their lives: ". . . the university Chapel is called to be a vital center for promoting the Christian renewal of culture, in respectful and frank dialogue, in a clear and well-grounded perspective (cf. 1 Pet. 3:15), in a witness which is open to questioning and capable of convincing" (*Address to the European Congress of University Chaplains*, May 1, 1998, no. 4). Young adults need the service of committed chaplains who can help them, intellectually and spiritually, to attain their full maturity in Christ.

8. Dear Brother Bishops: on the threshold of a new century and a new millennium, the Church continues to proclaim the capacity of human beings to know the truth and to grow into genuine freedom through their acceptance of that truth. In this respect, the Church is the defender of the moral insight on which your country was founded. Your Catholic schools are widely recognized as models for the renewal of American elementary and secondary education. Your Catholic colleges and universities can be leaders in the renewal of American higher education. At a time when the relationship between freedom and moral truth is being debated on a host of issues at every level of society and government, Catholic scholars have the resources to contribute to an intellectual and moral renewal of American culture. As you work to strengthen Catholic education, and as you promote Catholic intellectual life in all its dimensions, may you enjoy the protection of the Blessed Virgin Mary, Seat of Wisdom. On the eve of the Feast of Pentecost, I join you in invoking the gifts of the Holy Spirit upon the Church in the United States. With affection in the Lord, I cordially impart my Apostolic Blessing to you and to the priests, religious and laity of your Dioceses.

— From the Vatican, May 30, 1998

VII

The Role of the Laity
in the Church's Saving Mission

Dear Brother Bishops,

1. With great joy in the Lord I welcome you, *the Pastors of the Church in the States of Minnesota, North Dakota and South Dakota*, on your *ad limina* visit. The theme of my reflections with the Bishops of your country this year is the duty, in view of the approaching new millennium, of renewed evangelization, for which the Second Vatican Council marvelously prepared the way. Today I wish to reflect on *the laity in the Church's life and mission*. The new evangelization that can make the twenty-first century a springtime of the Gospel is a task for the entire People of God, but will depend in a decisive way on the lay faithful being fully aware of their baptismal vocation and their responsibility for bringing the good news of Jesus Christ to their culture and society.

The Fathers of the Second Vatican Council gave special attention to the dignity and mission of the lay faithful, urging them "in the Lord's name to give a glad, generous and prompt response to the impulse of the Holy Spirit and to the voice of Christ, who is giving them an especially urgent invitation at this moment" (*Apostolicam Actuositatem*, 33). In order to restore the needed balance to ecclesial life, the Council dedicated an extremely rich chapter in *Lumen Gentium* to *the role of the laity in the Church's saving mission*, and it further developed this theme in the Decree on the Apostolate of the Laity (*Apostolicam Actuositatem*). With specific reference to contemporary circumstances, that mission was specified still more concretely in the Pastoral Constitution on the Church in the Modern World (*Gaudium et Spes*). In these documents and others the Council sought to extend the great flourishing of the lay apostolate which had characterized previous decades. More and more lay people had taken to heart the stirring words of Pope Pius XII: "Lay believers are in the front line of Church life; for them the Church is the animating principle of human society. Therefore, they in particular ought to have an ever clearer consciousness not only of belonging to the Church, but of being the Church" (*Discourse*, February 20, 1946).

2. It was in this context of vigorous lay action that the Council could clearly affirm: "It is evident to everyone that all the faithful of Christ of whatever rank or status are called to the fullness of the Christian life and to the perfection of charity" (*Lumen Gentium*, 40); and the Council's Decree on the Apostolate of the Laity makes it clear that lay people are called to exercise the apostolate *in the Church and in the world* (cf. *Apostolicam Actuositatem*, 5). Lay men and women have indeed responded to this call. Everywhere there has been a blossoming of various forms of lay participation in the Church's life and mission. Much has also been done since the Council to explore more deeply *the theological basis for the vocation and mission of the laity*. This development reached a certain maturity in the 1987 Synod of Bishops on the role of the Laity, with

the subsequent Post-Synodal Apostolic Exhortation *Christifideles Laici*, published on December 30, 1988. The Synod indicated the concrete ways in which the Council's rich *teaching* on the lay state could be further translated into *practice*. One of its principal achievements was to set the various ministries and charisms within the framework of an ecclesiology of communion (cf. *Christifideles Laici*, 21). Thus it dealt with the specific role of the laity, not as an extension or derivation of the clerical and hierarchical role, but in relation to the fundamental truth that *all the baptized receive the same sanctifying grace*, the grace of justification by which each one becomes a "new creature," an adopted child of God, a "partaker of the divine nature," a member of Christ and co-heir with him, a temple of the Holy Spirit (cf. *Catechism of the Catholic Church*, 1265). All the faithful — both ordained ministers and laity — together form the one body of the Lord: "Here there cannot be Greek and Jew, circumcised and uncircumcised, barbarian, Scythian, slave, free man, but Christ is all, and in all" (Col. 3:11).

We are witnessing a return to the authentic *theology of the laity* found in the New Testament, where the Church, the body of Christ, is the whole of the chosen race, the royal priesthood, the holy nation, God's own people (cf. 1 Pet. 2:9), and not a portion of it. Saint Paul reminds us that *the growth of the body depends on every member playing its part*: "If we live by the truth and in love, we shall grow in all ways into Christ, who is the head, by whom the whole body is fitted and joined together, every joint adding its own strength, for each separate part to work according to its function. So the body grows until it has built itself up, in love" (Eph. 4:15–16). In preparing for the great ecclesial event that was the Second Vatican Council, Pope

John XXIII was so struck by these words that he declared that they deserved to be inscribed on the Council's doors (cf. *Address on Pentecost Sunday*, June 5, 1960).

In an ecclesiology of communion, the Church's hierarchical structure is not a matter of *power* but of *service*, completely ordered to the holiness of Christ's members. The threefold duty to teach, sanctify and govern, entrusted to Peter and the Apostles and their successors, "has no other purpose except to form the Church in line with the ideal of sanctity already programmed and prefigured in Mary" (*Address to the Roman Curia*, 22 December 1987, no. 3). The Marian dimension of the Church is prior to the Petrine or hierarchical dimension, "as well as being supreme and pre-eminent, richer in personal and communitarian implications for the various ecclesial vocations" (*ibid.*). If I mention these well-known truths, it is because everywhere in the Church, and not least in your country, we see the spread of *a fresh and invigorating lay spirituality* and the magnificent fruits of the laity's greater involvement in the Church's life. As we approach the Third Christian Millennium it is of paramount importance that the Pope and the Bishops, fully conscious of their own special ministry of service in the Mystical Body of Christ, continue to "stir and promote a deeper awareness among all the faithful of the gift and responsibility they share, both in association and as individuals, in the communion and mission of the Church" (*Christifideles Laici*, 2).

3.   The liturgical renewal which the Council ardently desired and fostered has resulted in *the more frequent and lively participation of the lay faithful in the tasks proper to them in the liturgical assembly*. Full, active and conscious

participation in the liturgy should give birth to a more vigorous lay witness in the world, not a confusion of roles in the worshiping community. Based on the will of Christ himself, there is a fundamental distinction between the ordained ministry arising from the Sacrament of Holy Orders, and the functions open to lay people, and founded on the Sacraments of Baptism, Confirmation and, for most, Matrimony. The intention of the Holy See's recent *Instruction on Certain Questions Regarding the Collaboration of the Non-Ordained Faithful in the Sacred Ministry of Priests* has been to reaffirm and clarify the canonical and disciplinary norms regulating this area, by putting the relevant directives in relation to the theological and ecclesiological principles involved. I urge you to ensure that the liturgical life of your communities is led and governed by the grace of Christ working through the Church, which the Lord intended as a hierarchical communion. The distinction between the priesthood of the faithful and the ministerial priesthood must always be respected, since it belongs to "the constitutive form which [Christ] indelibly impressed on his Church" (*Discourse at the Symposium on "The Participation of the Lay Faithful in the Priestly Ministry,"* April 22, 1994, no. 5).

4. As the Fathers at the 1987 Synod on the Laity pointed out, it is an inadequate understanding of the role of the laity which leads lay men and women to become so strongly interested in Church services and tasks that they fail to become actively involved in their responsibilities in the professional, social, cultural and political field (cf. *Christifideles Laici*, 2). The first requirement of the new evangelization is *the actual witness of Christians who live by*

the Gospel: "Let your light so shine before men, that they may see your good works and give glory to your Father who is in heaven" (Matt. 5:16). Since lay people are at the forefront of the Church's mission to evangelize all areas of human activity — including the workplace, the worlds of science and medicine, the world of politics, and the diverse world of culture — they must be strong enough and sufficiently catechized "to testify how the Christian faith constitutes the only valid response . . . to the problems and hopes that life poses to every person and society" (*Christifideles Laici*, 34). As my predecessor Pope Paul VI put it: "Take a Christian or a handful of Christians who in the midst of their own community show their capacity for understanding and acceptance, their sharing of life and destiny with other people, their solidarity with the efforts of all for whatever is noble and good. Let us suppose that, in addition, they radiate in an altogether simple and unaffected way their faith in values that go beyond current values, and their hope in something that is not seen and that one would not dare to imagine. Through this wordless witness these Christians stir up irresistible questions in the hearts of those who see how they live: Why are they like this? Why do they live in this way? What or who is it that inspires them? Why are they in our midst? Such a witness is already a silent proclamation of the Good News and a very powerful and effective one" (*Evangelii Nuntiandi*, 21). Through God's grace, your particular Churches are all gifted with Catholic men and women eager to live a full Christian life and to work for Christ's kingdom in the world around them. The Bishops must not fail them by a lack of pastoral leadership. In your ministry and governance you have to impress on everyone the importance of formation and adult catechesis, prayer and sacramental practice, a real commitment to the evangelization of culture and the application of Christian moral and social doctrine in public and private life.

5. *The immediate and in many ways most important arena of the laity's Christian witness is marriage and the family.* Where family life is strong and healthy, the sense of community and solidarity is also strong, and this helps to build that "civilization of life and love" which must be everyone's aim. But where the family is weak, all human relationships are exposed to instability and fragmentation. Today the family is under pressure from many quarters: "The family is placed at the center of the great struggle between good and evil, between life and death, between love and all that is opposed to love. To the family is entrusted the task of striving, first and foremost, to unleash the forces of good, the source of which is found in Christ the Redeemer of man" (cf. *Letter to Families*, 23). At a time when the very definitions of marriage and family are endangered by attempts to enshrine in legislation alternative and distorted notions of these basic human communities, your ministry must include the clear proclamation of the truth of God's original design.

Since the Christian family is the "domestic church," couples must be helped to relate their family life in concrete ways to the life and mission of the Church (cf. *Familiaris Consortio*, 49). The parish should be a "family of families," helping in every way possible to nourish the spiritual life of parents and children through prayer, the word of God, the sacraments, and the witness of holiness and charity. Bishops and priests should be eager to help and encourage families in every way, and should give their support to groups and associations which promote family life. While it is important that the local Church respond to the needs of people in problem situations, pastoral planning should also give adequate attention to the needs of ordinary families seeking to live up to their vocation. These families are the backbone of society and the hope of the Church: the principal promoters of Christian family life are couples and families themselves, who have a special responsibility to be servants of other couples and families.

6. This year marks the thirtieth anniversary of the publication by my predecessor Pope Paul VI of the Encyclical Letter *Humanae Vitae*. The truth about human sexuality, and the Church's teaching on the sanctity of human life and on responsible parenthood, must be presented in the light of the theological development which has followed that document, and *in the light of the experience of couples who have faithfully followed this teaching*. Many couples have experienced how natural family planning promotes mutual respect, encourages tenderness between husband and wife, and helps develop an authentic inner freedom (cf. *Catechism of the Catholic Church*, 2370; *Humanae Vitae*, 21). Their experience deserves to be shared, for it is the living confirmation of the truth which *Humanae Vitae* teaches. In contrast, there is a growing awareness of the serious harm caused to marital relationships by recourse to artificial contraception, which, because it inevitably thwarts the total self-giving implied in the conjugal act, at one and the same time destroys its procreative meaning and weakens its unitive significance (cf. *Evangelium Vitae*, 13).

With courage and compassion, Bishops, priests and lay Catholics must seize the opportunity to propose to the sons and daughters of the Church, and to the whole of society, the truth about the special gift that is human sexuality. The false promises of the "sexual revolution" are now painfully obvious in the human suffering caused by unprecedented rates of divorce, by the scourge of abortion and its lasting effects on those involved. Yet the teaching of the Magisterium, the development of the "theology of the body," and the experience of faithful Catholic couples have given Catholics in the United States a uniquely powerful and compelling opportunity to bring the truth about human sexuality into a society that sorely needs to hear it.

7. The *multi-cultural reality of American society* is a source of enrichment for the Church, but it also presents challenges to pastoral action. Many Dioceses, because of past and continuing immigration, have a strong Hispanic presence. The Hispanic faithful bring their own particular gifts to the local Church, not least the vitality of their faith and their deep sense of family values. They also face enormous difficulties, and you are making great efforts to have priests and others appropriately trained to provide good pastoral care and needed services to minority families and communities. In the face of extremely active proselytism by other religious groups, instruction in the faith, the building up of living communities, attention to the needs of families and young people, the fostering of personal and family prayer, a spiritual and liturgical life centered on the Eucharist and genuine Marian devotion are all essential (cf. *Address to Hispanics at Our Lady of Guadalupe Plaza, San*

Antonio, September 13, 1987). The Hispanic faithful should be able to feel that their natural place, their spiritual home, is in the heart of the Catholic community.

The same should be said about the members of the African-American community, who also are a vital presence in all your Churches. Their love for the word of God is a special blessing to be treasured. While the United States has made great progress in ridding itself of racial prejudice, continuous efforts are needed to ensure that black Catholics are fully involved in the Church's life.

In your Dioceses, as in other parts of the United States, there are not a few Native Americans, proud descendants of the original peoples of your land. I encourage your efforts to provide for their spiritual care, to support them as they strive to preserve the good and noble traditions of their culture, and to be close to them as they struggle to overcome the negative effects of the marginalization from which they have suffered for so long. In the one Church of Christ, every culture and race finds its home.

8. Finally, I wish to tell you of the great joy which I experienced last weekend in Saint Peter's Square at the meeting of so many lay members of the various ecclesial movements and communities which represent a providential gift of the Holy Spirit to the Church of our time. These movements and communities share a strong commitment to the spiritual life and to missionary outreach. As instruments of conversion and authentic Gospel witness, they render a magnificent service in helping the Church's members to respond to the universal call to holiness and to their vocation to transform worldly realities in the light of the Gospel values of life, freedom and love. They repre-

sent a genuine source of renewal and evangelization, and should therefore have an important place in your discernment and pastoral planning.

An extraordinary and surprising new springtime for the Church will blossom from the dynamic faith, living hope and active charity of the lay men and women who open their hearts to the life-giving presence of the Holy Spirit. As Bishops our task is to teach, sanctify and govern in the name of Christ, seeking always to bring to fruition the gifts and talents of the faithful entrusted to our care. I urge you to encourage everyone to take their proper place in the Church and to become ever more personally responsible for her mission. Devote special attention to strengthening family life, as the essential condition of the well-being of individuals and society. Draw on the spiritual resources of the various cultures present in the Church in the United States, and direct them to the genuine renewal of the whole People of God. Entrusting your episcopal ministry to the intercession of Mary, Help of Christians, I pray for the priests, religious and lay faithful of your Dioceses and I cordially impart my Apostolic Blessing.

— From the Vatican, June 5, 1998

VIII

Consecrated Persons
at the Heart of the Church

Dear Brother Bishops,

1. On the occasion of your *ad limina* visit, I warmly welcome you, the Pastors of *the Church in the ecclesiastical region of Saint Louis, Omaha, Dubuque and Kansas City.* Through you I greet the priests, religious and lay faithful of your Dioceses: "Grace, mercy, and peace from God the Father and Christ Jesus our Lord" (1 Tim. 1:2). Continuing the theme of these *ad limina* talks, today it is my intention to devote my remarks to *the reality of the consecrated life* in the Churches over which you and your Brother Bishops preside in charity and pastoral service. These brief reflections aim neither to be a full presentation of the consecrated life nor to address all the practical questions which come up in your relations with religious. Rather, I wish to support you in your ministry as Successors of the Apostles, a ministry which extends also to the consecrated persons living and working in your Dioceses.

In particular, I wish to express a special word of appreciation, gratitude and encouragement to the women and men who, *through the observance of the evangelical counsels, make visible in the Church the form that the Incarnate Son of God took upon himself during his earthly life* (cf. *Vita Con-*

secrata, 14). By their consecration and fraternal life, they bear witness to the new creation inaugurated by Christ and made possible in us through the power of the Holy Spirit. By their prayer and sacrifice, they sustain the Church's fidelity to her saving mission. By their solidarity with the poor, they imitate the compassion of Jesus himself and his love of justice. By their intellectual apostolates, they serve the proclamation of the Gospel in the heart of the world's cultures. By giving their lives to the hardest tasks, countless consecrated women and men in the United States, and all over the world, testify to the supremacy of God and the ultimate significance of Jesus Christ for human life. Many of them are involved in missionary work, especially in Latin America, Africa and Asia, and in recent times some of them have borne the ultimate witness by shedding their blood for the Gospel's sake. The witness of consecrated persons makes tangible in the midst of God's People the spirit of the Beatitudes, the value of the great commandment of love of God and love of neighbor. In a word, *consecrated persons are at the very heart of the mystery of the Church*, the Bride who responds to Christ's infinite love with her whole being. How could we Bishops fail to praise God unceasingly and be filled with gratitude for such a gift to his Church!

2. The gift of consecrated life forms an integral part of the pastoral solicitude of the Successor of Peter and of the Bishops. The indivisibility of the Bishops' pastoral ministry means that they have a specific *responsibility for overseeing all charisms and callings*, and this translates into specific duties regarding the consecrated life as it exists in each particular Church (cf. *Mutuae Relationes*, 9). Religious

Institutes for their part ought to be eager to establish a cordial and effective cooperation with the Bishops (cf. *ibid.*, 13), who by divine institution have succeeded the Apostles as shepherds of the Church, so that whoever hears them hears Christ (cf. Luke 10:16; *Lumen Gentium*, 20). *The new springtime which the Church confidently awaits must also be a time of renewal and even re-birth of the consecrated life!* The seeds of renewal are already showing many promising results, and the new Institutes of consecrated life now taking their place alongside the older ones bear witness to the abiding relevance and appeal of the total gift of self to the Lord according to the charisms of the Founders and Foundresses.

3. Over a considerable period religious life in the United States has been characterized by change and adaptation, as called for by the Second Vatican Council and codified in Canon Law and other magisterial documents. This has not been an easy time, since a renewal of such complexity and far-reaching consequences, involving so many people, could not take place without much effort and strain. It has not always been easy to strike a proper balance between necessary change and fidelity to the spiritual and canonical experience which had become a stable and fruitful part of the Church's living tradition. All of this has sometimes resulted in suffering for individual religious and for whole communities, a suffering which in some cases has brought new insights and a new commitment but which in other cases has resulted in disenchantment and discouragement. Ever since the beginning of my Pontificate I have tried to encourage the Bishops to engage religious communities

in a dialogue of faith and fidelity, with the aim of *helping religious to live their ecclesial vocation to the full*. Down the years I have many times discussed the state of religious life in your country with religious themselves, as well as with the Bishops and others concerned. In all the initiatives undertaken in this regard, it has been my intention on the one hand to affirm *the personal and collegial responsibility for religious life* which belongs to the Bishops as the ones primarily responsible for the Church's holiness, doctrine and mission, and on the other to affirm the importance and value of the consecrated life, and *the extraordinary merits of so many consecrated women and men in every kind of service, at the side of suffering humanity*.

Today I wish to invite the United States Bishops to continue to foster personal contacts with the religious actually living and working in the individual Dioceses in order to encourage and challenge them. Generally speaking your relations with religious are truly friendly and cooperative, and in many cases they play an important part in your pastoral plans and projects. It is a matter of confirming that relationship *in its natural setting, the context of dynamic communion with the local Church*. The mission of religious places them in a definite particular Church: their vocation to serve the universal Church, then, is exercised within the structures of the particular Church (cf. *Address to Superiors General*, November 24, 1978). This is an important point, for many errors of judgement can result when a sound ecclesiology gives way to a concept of the Church too marked by civil and political terms, or so "spiritualized" that the individual's subjective choices become the criteria of behavior.

4. As Bishops you have a duty to safeguard and proclaim the values of religious life, in order that they may be faithfully preserved and passed on within the life of your diocesan communities. Poverty and self-possession, consecrated chastity and fruitfulness, obedience and freedom: these paradoxes proper to the consecrated life need to be better understood and more fully appreciated by the whole Church, and in particular by those who have a part in educating the faithful. The theology and spirituality of the consecrated life need to be a part of the training of diocesan priests, just as attention to the theology of the particular Church and to the spirituality of the diocesan clergy should be included in the formation of consecrated persons (cf. *Vita Consecrata*, 50).

In your contacts with religious, you will point to *the importance of their community witness* and show your willingness to help in whatever way possible to ensure that communities have the spiritual and material means to live the common life serenely and joyfully (cf. Congregation for Institutes of Consecrated Life and Societies of Apostolic Life, *Fraternal Life in Community*, February 2, 1994). One of the most valuable services that a Bishop can provide is to ensure that good and experienced spiritual guides and confessors are available to religious, especially to monasteries of contemplative nuns and motherhouses with many members. Likewise, an Institute's capacity to conduct *a common or community apostolate* is of vital concern to the life of a particular Church. It is not enough that all members of an Institute subscribe to the same general values, or work "according to the founding spirit," with each one responsible for finding some place of apostolic activity and a residence. Obviously not every member of an Institute will be suited to work in only one apostolate, but the identity and nature of the common apostolate, and the willingness to engage in it, should be an essential part of an Institute's discerning of the vocation of its candidates. Only when a Diocese can rely on a religious Institute's commitment to a community apostolate can it engage seriously in long-range pastoral planning. Where Institutes are already engaged in community apostolates such as education and health care, they should be encouraged and helped to persevere. Sensitivity to new needs and to the new poor, however necessary and laudable, should not entail neglect of the old poor, those in need of genuine Catholic education, the sick and the elderly. You should also encourage religious to give explicit attention to the specifically Catholic dimension of their activities. Only on this basis will Catholic schools and centers of higher learning be able to promote a culture imbued with Catholic values and morality; only in this way will Catholic health-care facilities ensure that the sick and needy are taken care of "for the sake of Christ" and according to Catholic moral and ethical principles.

5. In many Dioceses consecrated life is facing the challenge of declining numbers and advancing age. The Bishops of the United States have already shown their readiness to lend assistance, and the Catholic faithful have demonstrated great generosity in providing financial support for religious Institutes with particular needs in this area. Religious communities themselves need to reaffirm their confidence in their calling and, relying on the help of the Holy Spirit, re-propose the ideal of consecration and mission. A presentation of the evangelical counsels merely in terms of their usefulness and convenience for a particular form of

service is not enough. It is *only personal experience, through faith, of Christ and of the mystery of his kingdom at work in human history* which can make the ideal come alive in the minds and hearts of those who may be called. At the approach of the new Millennium, the Church urgently needs a vital and appealing religious life that *shows forth concretely the sovereignty of God* and bears witness before the world to *the transcendent value of the "total gift of self in the profession of the evangelical counsels"* (*Vita Consecrata*, 16), a gift which overflows in contemplation and service. This is surely the kind of challenge to which young people will respond. If it is true that the person becomes himself or herself through the sincere gift of self (cf. *Gaudium et Spes*, 24), then there should be no hesitation in calling the young to consecration. It is in fact a call to full human and Christian maturity and fulfilment.

Perhaps the Great Jubilee might be an occasion for Institutes of consecrated life to set up and support new communities of their members who are seeking an authentic, stable and community centered experience according to the spirit of the Founders and Foundresses. In many cases this would permit religious to commit themselves more serenely to these goals, free from burdens and problems which ultimately cannot be resolved.

6. The two-thousandth anniversary of the birth of the Savior invites the whole Church to be *absorbed with bringing Christ to the world*. She must proclaim his victory over sin and death, a victory brought about in his Blood on the Cross, and every day made truly present in the Eucharist. We know that genuine hope for the future of the human family lies in presenting clearly to the world the incarnate

Son of God as the exemplar of all human life. Religious in particular should be ready to make this proclamation in openness to the sanctifying power of the Holy Spirit and with complete inner freedom from any residual fear of displeasing the "world," understood as a culture which promises a liberation and salvation different from those of Christ. This is no vain triumphalism or presumption, for in every age Christ is "the power of God and the wisdom of God" (1 Cor. 1:24). In our day, as throughout the history of the Church, consecrated women and men stand out as living icons of what it means to make the following of Jesus the whole purpose of one's life and to be transformed by his grace. In fact, as the Apostolic Exhortation *Vita Consecrata* points out: religious "have set out on a journey of continual conversion, of exclusive dedication to the love of God and of [their] brothers and sisters, in order to bear ever more splendid witness to the grace which transfigures Christian life" (no. 109). Because Christ will never fail his Church, religious have "not only a glorious history to remember and to recount, but also *a great history still to be accomplished!*" (*ibid.*, 110).

Dear Brother Bishops, through you I earnestly exhort the women and men religious who have borne the "burden of the day and the scorching heat" (Matt. 20:12) to persevere in their faithful witness. There is a way of living the Cross with bitterness and sadness, but it breaks our spirit. There is also the way of carrying the Cross as Christ did, and then we perceive clearly that it leads "into glory" (cf. Luke 24:26). Through you, I appeal to all consecrated persons, and to the men and women who may be thinking of entering a community, to renew each day their awareness of the extraordinary privilege that is theirs: the call to serve the holiness of God's People, *to "be holiness" in the heart of the Church.*

With your leadership and guidance, the future of the consecrated life in your country will certainly be glorious and fruitful. May the Blessed Virgin Mary who, since she belongs completely to God and is totally devoted to him, is the sublime example of perfect consecration accompany the renewal and the new flourishing of the consecrated life in the United States. To you and to the priests, religious and laity of your Dioceses, I cordially impart my Apostolic Blessing.

— From the Vatican, June 13, 1998

IX

Freedom and the Moral Law

Dear Brother Bishops,

1. I warmly welcome you, the Pastors of the Church in *the States of Texas, Oklahoma and Arkansas*, on the occasion of your *ad limina* visit. In my meetings so far this year with the United States Bishops, we have considered some principal aspects of the new evangelization called for by the Second Vatican Council, the great event of grace by which the Holy Spirit has prepared the Church to enter the Third Christian Millennium. One essential part of this task is *the proclamation of moral truth* and its application to the personal lives of Christians and to their involvement in the world. Therefore, I wish to reflect with you today on your episcopal ministry as *teachers of moral truth and witnesses to the moral law*.

In every age, men and women need to hear Christ the Good Shepherd calling them to faith and conversion of life (cf. Mark 1:15). As shepherds of souls, you must be Christ's voice today, encouraging your people to rediscover "the beauty of truth, the liberating force of God's love, and the value of unconditional fidelity to all the demands of the Lord's law, even in the most difficult situations" (*Veritatis Splendor*, 107). The question posed by the rich young man in the Gospel — "Teacher, what good must I do to have eternal life?" (Matt. 19:16) — is a perennial human question. It is asked in one form or another, explicitly or implicitly, by every human being in every culture and at every moment in the drama of history. Christ's answer to that question — to follow him in *doing the will of his Father — is the key to the fullness of life which he promises*. Obedience to God's commandments, far from alienating us from our humanity, is the pathway to genuine liberation and the source of true happiness.

In this year of preparation for the Great Jubilee dedicated to the Holy Spirit, let us remember that our efforts to preach the Good News and teach the moral truth about the human person are sustained by the Spirit, who is the principal agent in the Church's mission (cf. *Evangelii Nuntiandi*, 75). It is the Holy Spirit who "brings about the flourishing of Christian moral life and the witness of holiness amid the great variety of vocations, gifts, responsibilities, conditions and life situations" (*Veritatis Splendor*, 108). In your Dioceses and parishes, I urge you to make a special effort this year to increase awareness of the powerful activity of the Spirit in the world, for it is through his grace that we experience a "radical personal and social renewal capable of ensuring justice, solidarity, honesty and openness" (*Veritatis Splendor*, 98).

2.   Given the circumstances of contemporary culture, your episcopal ministry is especially challenging, and the situation which you face as teachers of moral truth is complex. Your parishes are filled with Catholics eager to lead responsible lives as spouses, parents, citizens, workers, and professionals. These men and women, whom you meet daily in the course of your pastoral mission, know that

they should live morally upright lives, but often they find it difficult to explain exactly what this implies. This difficulty reflects another side of contemporary culture: the skepticism regarding the very existence of "moral truth" and an objective moral law. This attitude is quite prevalent in the cultural institutions that influence public opinion, and, it must be said, is commonplace in many of your country's academic, political and legal structures. In this situation, those who try to live according to the moral law often feel pressured by forces which contradict the things they know in their hearts to be true. And those responsible for teaching moral truth may feel as if their task is virtually impossible, given the power of those external cultural pressures.

There have been similar moments in the course of the Church's two-thousand-year history. Yet *today's cultural crisis has distinctive characteristics that give your task as moral teachers a real urgency*. This urgency touches both the transmission of the moral truth contained in the Gospel and the Magisterium of the Church, and the future of society as a free and democratic way of life.

How should we define this crisis of moral culture? We can glimpse its first phase in what Cardinal John Henry Newman wrote in his *Letter to the Duke of Norfolk*: "In this century [conscience] has been superseded by a counterfeit, which the eighteen centuries prior to it never heard of, and could not have mistaken for it, if they had. It is the right of self-will." What was true in Newman's nineteenth century is even truer today. Culturally powerful forces insist that the rights of conscience are violated by the very idea that there exists a moral law inscribed in our humanity, which we can come to know by reflecting on our nature and our actions, and which lays certain obligations upon us because we recognize them as universally true and binding. This, it is frequently said, is an abrogation of freedom. But what is the concept of "freedom" at work here? Is freedom merely an assertion of my will — "I should be permitted to do this because *I* choose to do it"? Or is freedom the right to do what I ought to do, to adhere freely to what is good and true (cf. *Homily at Baltimore*, October 8, 1995)?

The notion of freedom as personal autonomy is superficially attractive; endorsed by intellectuals, the media, legislatures, and the courts, it becomes a powerful cultural force. Yet it ultimately destroys the personal good of individuals and the common good of society. Freedom-as-autonomy, by its single-minded focus on the autonomous will of the individual as the sole organizing principle of public life, dissolves the bonds of obligation between men and women, parents and children, the strong and the weak, majorities and minorities. The result is the breakdown of civil society, and a public life in which the only actors of consequence are the autonomous individual and the state. This, as the twentieth century ought to have taught us, is a sure prescription for tyranny.

3. At its roots, the contemporary crisis of moral culture is a crisis of understanding of the nature of the human person. As pastors and teachers of the Church of Christ, you remind people that the greatness of human beings is founded precisely in their being creatures of a loving God, who gave them the capacity to know the good and to choose it, and who sent his Son to be the final and unsurpassable witness to the truth about the human condition: "In Christ and through Christ, God has revealed himself

fully to mankind and has definitively drawn close to it; at the same time, in Christ and through Christ man has acquired full awareness of his dignity, of the heights to which he is raised, of the surpassing worth of his own humanity, and of the meaning of his existence" (*Redemptor Hominis*, 11). In Christ, we know that "the good of the person lies in being in the Truth and *doing* the Truth" (*Address to the International Congress of Moral Theology*, April 10, 1986, no. 1).

In this Christian anthropology, the nobility of men and women lies, not simply in the capacity to *choose*, but in *the capacity to choose wisely and to live according to that choice of what is good*. In all of visible creation, only the human person chooses reflectively. Only the human person can discern between good and evil, and give reasons justifying that discernment. Only human beings can make sacrifices for what is good and true. That is why, throughout Christian history, the martyr remains the paradigm of discipleship: for the martyr lives out the relationship between truth, freedom, and goodness in the most radical way.

By teaching the moral truth about the human person and witnessing to the moral law inscribed on the human heart, *the Bishops of the Church are defending and promoting not arbitrary claims made by the Church but essential truths, and therefore the good of individuals and the common good of society.*

4. If the dignity of the human person as a moral agent rests on the capacity to know and choose what is truly good, then *the question of conscience comes into clearer focus*. Respect for the rights of conscience is deeply ingrained in your national culture, which was formed in part by emigrants

who came to the New World to vindicate their religious and moral convictions in the face of persecution. American society's historic admiration for men and women of conscience is the ground on which you can teach the truth about conscience today.

The Church honors conscience as the "sanctuary" of the human person: here, men and women are "alone with God," whose voice echoes in the depths of their hearts, summoning them to love good and avoid evil (cf. *Gaudium et Spes*, 16). Conscience is that inner place where "man detects a law which he does not impose upon himself, but which holds him to obedience" (*ibid.*). This being the case, the dignity of conscience is demeaned when it is suggested, as the defenders of radical individual autonomy claim, that conscience is a wholly independent, exclusively personal capacity to determine what constitutes good and evil (cf. *Dominum et Vivificantem*, 43).

Everyone must act in accordance with conscience. But *conscience is neither absolutely independent nor infallible in its judgments*; if it were, conscience would be reduced to the mere assertion of personal will. Thus it is precisely a defense of the dignity of conscience and of the human person to teach that consciences must be *formed*, so that they can discern what actually does or does not correspond to the "eternal, objective and universal divine law" which human intelligence is capable of discovering in the order of being (cf. *Dignitatis Humanae*, 3; *Veritatis Splendor*, 60). *Because of the nature of conscience*, the admonition always to follow it must immediately be followed by the question of whether what our conscience is telling us is true or not. If we fail to make this necessary clarification, conscience — instead of being that holy place where God reveals to us our true good — becomes a force which is destructive of our true humanity and of all our relationships (cf. *General Audience*, August 17, 1983, no. 3). *As Bishops you have to teach that freedom of conscience is never freedom from the truth but always and only freedom in the truth.* This understanding of conscience and its relationship to freedom should clarify certain aspects of the question of dissent from Church teaching. By the will of Christ himself and the life-giving power of the Holy Spirit, the Church is preserved in the truth and "it is her duty to give utterance to, and authoritatively to teach, that truth which is Christ himself, and to declare and confirm by her authority those principles of the moral order which have their origin in human nature itself" (*Dignitatis Humanae*, 14). When the Church teaches, for example, that abortion, sterilization or euthanasia are always morally inadmissible, she is giving expression to the universal moral law inscribed on the human heart, and is therefore teaching something which is binding on everyone's conscience. *Her absolute prohibition that such procedures be carried out in Catholic health care facilities* is simply an act of fidelity to God's law. As Bishops you must remind everyone involved — hospital administrations and medical personnel — that any failure to comply with this prohibition is both a grievous sin and a source of scandal (for sterilizations cf. Congregation for the Doctrine of the Faith, *Quaecumque sterilizatio*, March 13, 1975, AAS [1976] 738–740). This and other such instances are not, it must be emphasized, the imposition of an *external* set of criteria in violation of human freedom. Rather, the Church's teaching of moral truth "brings to light the truths which [conscience] ought already to possess" (*Veritatis Splendor*, 64), and it is these truths which make us free in the deepest meaning of human freedom and give our humanity its genuine nobility.

Almost two thousand years ago, Saint Paul urged us to "not be conformed to this world" but to live the true freedom that is obedience to the will of God (Rom. 12:2). In teaching the truth about conscience and its intrinsic relationship to moral truth, you will be challenging one of the great forces in the modern world. But at the same time, you will be doing the modern world a great service, for you will be reminding it of the only foundation capable of sustaining a culture of freedom: what the Founders of your nation called "self-evident" truths.

5. From this perspective, it should be clear that the Church addresses issues of public life not for political reasons but as *a servant of the truth about the human person, a defender of human dignity and a promoter of human freedom.* A society or culture which wishes to survive cannot declare the spiritual dimension of the human person to be irrelevant to public life. Cultures develop as ways of dealing with the most profound experiences of human existence: love, birth, friendship, work, death. Each of these experiences raises, in its unique way, the question of God: "at the heart of every culture lies the attitude man takes to the greatest mystery: the mystery of God" (*Centesimus Annus*, 24). American Catholics, in common with other Christians and all believers, have a responsibility to ensure that the mystery of God and the truth about humanity that is revealed in the mystery of God are not banished from public life.

This is especially important for democratic societies, since one of the truths contained in the mystery of our creation by God is that the human person must be "the origin, the subject and the purpose of all social institutions" (*Gaudium et Spes*, 25). Our intrinsic dignity and inalienable fundamental rights are not the result of social convention: they precede all social conventions and provide the norms that determine their validity. The history of the twentieth century is a grim warning of the evils that result when human beings are reduced to the status of objects to be manipulated by the powerful for selfish gain or for ideological reasons. In proclaiming the truth that God has given men and women an inestimable dignity and inalienable rights from the moment of conception, you are helping to rebuild the moral foundations of a genuine culture of freedom, capable of sustaining institutions of self-governance that serve the common good.

6. It is a tribute to the Church and to the openness of American society that so many Catholics in the United States are involved in political life. As pastors and teachers, your responsibility to Catholic public officials is to remind them of the heritage of reflection on the moral law, on society, on democracy, which they ought to bring to their office.

Your country prides itself on being a realized democracy, but democracy is itself a moral adventure, a continuing test of a people's capacity to govern themselves in ways that serve the common good and the good of individual citizens. The survival of a particular democracy depends not only on its institutions, but to an even greater extent on the spirit which inspires and permeates its procedures for legislating, administering, and judging. *The future of democracy in fact depends on a culture capable of forming men and women who are prepared to defend certain truths and values*. It is imperiled when politics and law are sundered from any connection to the moral law written on the human heart.

If there is no objective standard to help adjudicate between different conceptions of the personal and common good, then democratic politics is reduced to a raw contest for power. If constitutional and statutory law are not held accountable to the objective moral law, the first casualties are justice and equity, for they become matters of personal opinion. Catholics in public life render a particularly important service to society when they defend objective moral norms as "the unshakable foundation and solid guarantee of a just and peaceful human coexistence, and hence of genuine democracy," for it is through our common obligation to these moral norms that we come to know, and can defend, the equality of all citizens, "who possess common rights and duties" (*Veritatis Splendor*, 96).

A climate of moral relativism is incompatible with democracy. That kind of culture cannot answer questions fundamental to a democratic political community: "Why should I regard my fellow citizen as my equal?"; "Why should I defend someone else's rights?"; "Why should I work for the common good?" *If moral truths cannot be publicly acknowledged as such, democracy is impossible* (cf. *Veritatis Splendor*, 101). Thus I wish to encourage you to continue to speak out clearly and effectively about the fundamental moral questions facing people today. The interest with which many of your documents have been received throughout society is an indication that you are providing much needed guidance when you remind everyone, and especially Catholic citizens and Catholic political leaders, of the essential bond between freedom and truth.

7. Dear Brother Bishops, a time of "crisis" is a time of opportunity as well as a time of danger. That is certainly true of the crisis of moral culture in the developed world today. The call of the Second Vatican Council to the People of God to witness to the truth about the human person amidst the joy and hope, grief and pain of the contemporary world is a call to all of us for *a personal commitment to effective episcopal leadership in the new evangelization*. By focusing the attention of the faithful and all your fellow citizens on the extremely serious moral choices before them, you will help to bring about that renewal of moral goodness, solidarity and genuine freedom which the United States and the world urgently need. Entrusting your ministry, and the priests, religious, and laity of your Dioceses to the protection of Mary, Patroness of the United States under the great title of her Immaculate Conception, I cordially impart my Apostolic Blessing.

— *From the Vatican, June 27, 1998*

X

Building a Culture of Life

Dear Cardinal Mahony,
Dear Brother Bishops,

1. With joy and affection I welcome you, *the Bishops of the Church in California, Nevada and Hawaii*, on the occasion of your visit *ad limina Apostolorum*. Your pilgrimage to the tombs of the Apostles Peter and Paul is a celebration of the ecclesial bonds linking your particular Churches to the See of Peter. Mindful that the Church throughout the world is preparing to celebrate the Great Jubilee of the Year 2000, I have chosen to devote this series of reflections with you and your Brother Bishops to the renewal of the Church's life envisaged by the Second Vatican Council. The Council was a gift of the Holy Spirit to the Church, and its full implementation is the best means of ensuring that the Catholic community in the United States enters the new millennium strengthened in faith and holiness, effectively contributing to a better society through its witness to the truth about man that is revealed in Jesus Christ (cf. *Gaudium et Spes*, 24). Indeed, the marvelous responsibility of the Church in your country is to spread this truth, which "enlightens man's intelligence and shapes his freedom, leading him to know and love the Lord" (*Veritatis Splendor*, Proem.)

We are coming to the end of a century which began

with confidence in humanity's prospects of almost unlimited progress, but which is now ending in widespread fear and moral confusion. If we want a springtime of the human spirit, we must rediscover the foundations of hope (cf. *Address to the 50th General Assembly of the United Nations Organization*, October 5, 1995, 16–18). Above all, society must learn to embrace once more the great gift of life, to cherish it, to protect it, and to defend it against the culture of death, itself an expression of the great fear that stalks our times. One of your most noble tasks as Bishops is *to stand firmly on the side of life, encouraging those who defend it and building with them a genuine culture of life.*

2. The Second Vatican Council was quite aware of the forces shaping contemporary society when it spoke out clearly in defense of human life against the many threats facing it (cf. *Gaudium et Spes*, 27). The Council also made a priceless contribution to *the culture of life* by its eloquent presentation of the full meaning of married love (cf. *ibid.*, 48–51). Following the lead of the Council and expounding its teaching, Pope Paul VI wrote the prophetic Encyclical *Humanae Vitae*, the thirtieth anniversary of which we are celebrating this year, in which he addressed the moral implications of *the power to cooperate with the Creator in bringing new life into the world.* The Creator has made man and woman to complement one another in love, and their union is no less than a sharing in the creative power of God himself. Conjugal love serves life not only insofar as it generates new life but also because, rightly understood as *the total gift of spouses to one another*, it shapes the loving and caring context in which new life is wholeheartedly welcomed as a gift of incomparable value.

Thirty years after *Humanae Vitae*, we see that mistaken

ideas about the individual's moral autonomy continue to inflict wounds on the consciences of many people and on the life of society. Paul VI pointed out some of the consequences of separating the unitive aspect of conjugal love from its procreative dimension: a gradual weakening of moral discipline; a trivialization of human sexuality; the demeaning of women; marital infidelity, often leading to broken families; state-sponsored programs of population control based on imposed contraception and sterilization (cf. *Humanae Vitae*, 17). The introduction of legalized abortion and euthanasia, ever increasing recourse to *in vitro* fertilization, and certain forms of genetic manipulation and embryo experimentation are also closely related in law and public policy, as well as in contemporary culture, to the idea of unlimited dominion over one's body and life.

The teaching of *Humanae Vitae* honors married love, promotes the dignity of women, and helps couples grow in understanding the truth of their particular path to holiness. It is also a response to contemporary culture's temptation to reduce life to a commodity. As Bishops, together with your priests, deacons, seminarians, and other pastoral personnel, you must find the right language and imagery to present this teaching in a comprehensible and compelling way. Marriage preparation programs should include an honest and complete presentation of the Church's teaching on responsible procreation, and should explain the natural methods of regulating fertility, the legitimacy of which is based on respect for the human meaning of sexual intimacy. Couples who have embraced the teaching of Pope Paul VI have discovered that it is truly a source of profound unity and joy, nourished by their increased mutual understanding and respect; they should be invited to share their experience with engaged couples taking part in marriage preparation programs.

3. Reflection on a very different anniversary serves to *heighten the sense of the urgency of the pro-life task*. In the twenty-five years which have passed since the judicial decision legalizing abortion in your country there has been a widespread mobilization of consciences in support of life. The pro-life movement is one of the most positive aspects of American public life, and the support given it by the Bishops is a tribute to your pastoral leadership. Despite the generous efforts of so many, however, the idea that elective abortion is a "right" continues to be asserted. Moreover, there are signs of an almost unimaginable insensitivity to the reality of what actually happens during an abortion, as evidenced in recent events surrounding so-called "partial-birth" abortion. This is a cause for deep concern. A society with a diminished sense of the value of human life at its earliest stages has already opened the door to a culture of death. As Pastors, you must make every effort to ensure that there is *no dulling of consciences regarding the seriousness of the crime of abortion*, a crime which cannot be morally justified by any circumstance, purpose or law (cf. *Evangelium Vitae*, 62).

Those who would defend life must make alternatives to abortion increasingly visible and available. Your recent pastoral statement, *Lights and Shadows*, draws attention to the need to support women in crisis pregnancies, and to provide counseling services for those who have had an abortion and must cope with its psychological and spiritual effects. Likewise, the unconditional defense of life must always include the message that true healing is possible, through reconciliation with the Body of Christ. In the spirit of the coming Great Jubilee of the Year 2000, American Catholics should be more than ever willing to open their hearts and their homes to "unwanted" and abandoned children, to young people in difficulty, to the handicapped and those who have no one to care for them.

4. The Church likewise offers a truly vital service to the nation when she awakens public awareness to the morally objectionable nature of campaigns for the legalization of physician-assisted suicide and euthanasia. *Euthanasia and suicide are grave violations of God's law* (cf. *Evangelium Vitae*, 65 and 66); their legalization introduces a direct threat to the persons least capable of defending themselves and it proves most harmful to the democratic institutions of society. The fact that Catholics have worked successfully with members of other Christian communities to resist efforts to legalize physician-assisted suicide is a very hopeful sign for the future of *ecumenical public witness in your country*, and I urge you to build an even broader ecumenical and inter-religious movement in defense of the culture of life and the civilization of love.

As ecumenical witness in defense of life develops, a great teaching effort is needed to clarify the substantive moral difference between discontinuing medical procedures that may be burdensome, dangerous or disproportionate to the expected outcome — what the *Catechism of the Catholic Church* calls "the refusal of 'over-zealous' treatment" (no. 2278; cf. *Evangelium Vitae*, 65) — and taking away the ordinary means of preserving life, such as feeding, hydration and normal medical care. The statement of the United States Bishops' Pro-Life Committee, *Nutrition and Hydration: Moral and Pastoral Considerations*, rightly emphasizes that the omission of nutrition and hydration intended to cause a patient's death must be rejected and that, while giving careful consideration to all the factors involved, the presumption should be in favor of providing medically assisted nutrition and hydration to all patients who need them. To blur this distinction is to introduce a source of countless injustices and much additional anguish, affecting both those already suffering from ill health or the deterioration which comes with age, and their loved ones.

5. In a culture that has difficulty in defining the meaning of life, death and suffering, the Christian message is the good news of Christ's victory over death and the certain hope of resurrection. The Christian accepts death as the supreme act of obedience to the Father, and is ready to meet death at the "hour" known only to him (cf. Mark 13:32). Life is a pilgrimage in faith to the Father, on which we travel in the company of his Son and the Saints in heaven. Precisely for this reason, the very real trial of suffering can become a source of good. Through suffering, we actually have a part in Christ's redemptive work for the Church and humanity (cf. *Salvifici Doloris*, 14–24). This is so when suffering is "experienced for love and with love through sharing, by God's gracious gift and one's own personal and free choice, in the suffering of Christ crucified" (*Evangelium Vitae*, 67).

The work of Catholic health care institutions in meeting the physical and spiritual needs of the sick is a form of imitation of Christ who, in the words of Saint Ignatius of Antioch, is "the doctor of the flesh and of the spirit" (*Ad Ephesios*, 7, 2). Doctors, nurses and other medical per-

sonnel deal with people in their time of trial, when they
have an acute sense of life's fragility and precariousness;
just when they most resemble the suffering Jesus in Geth-
semane and on Calvary. Health care professionals should
always bear in mind that their work is directed to individuals, unique persons in whom God's image is present in
a singular way and in whom he has invested his infinite
love. The sickness of a family member, friend or neighbor
is a call to Christians to demonstrate true compassion, that
gentle and persevering sharing in another's pain. Likewise,
the handicapped and those who are ill must never feel that
they are a burden; they are persons being visited by the
Lord. The terminally ill in particular deserve the solidarity, communion and affection of those around them; they
often need to be able to forgive and to be forgiven, to make
peace with God and with others. All priests should appreciate the pastoral importance of celebrating the Sacrament
of the Anointing of the Sick, particularly when it is the
prelude to the final journey to the Father's house: when
its meaning as the *sacramentum exeuntium* is particularly
evident (cf. *Catechism of the Catholic Church*, 1523).

6. An essential feature of support for the inalienable
right to life, from conception to natural death, is *the effort
to provide legal protection for the unborn, the handicapped,
the elderly, and those suffering from terminal illness*. As Bishops, you must continue to draw attention to the relationship of the moral law to constitutional and positive law
in your society: "Laws which legitimize the direct killing
of innocent human beings . . . are in complete opposition
to the inviolable right to life proper to every individual;
they thus deny the equality of everyone before the law"

(*Evangelium Vitae*, 72). What is at stake here is nothing less than the indivisible truth about the human person on which the Founding Fathers staked your nation's claim to independence. The life of a country is much more than its material development and its power in the world. A nation needs a "soul." It needs the wisdom and courage to overcome the moral ills and spiritual temptations inherent in its march through history. In union with all those who favor a "culture of life" over a "culture of death," Catholics, and especially Catholic legislators, must continue to make their voices heard in the formulation of cultural, economic, political and legislative projects which, "with respect for all and in keeping with democratic principles, will contribute to the building of a society in which the dignity of each person is recognized and the lives of all are defended and enhanced" (*Evangelium Vitae*, 90). Democracy stands or falls with the values which it embodies and promotes (cf. *Evangelium Vitae*, 70). In defending life you are defending an original and vital part of the vision on which your country was built. America must become, again, a hospitable society, in which every unborn child and every handicapped or terminally ill person is cherished and enjoys the protection of the law.

7. Dear Brother Bishops, *Catholic moral teaching is an essential part of our heritage of faith*; we must see to it that it is faithfully transmitted, and take appropriate measures to guard the faithful from the deceit of opinions which dissent from it (cf. *Veritatis Splendor*, 26 and 113). Although the Church often appears as a sign of contradiction, in defending the whole moral law firmly and humbly *she is upholding truths which are indispensable for the good of humanity*

and for the safeguarding of civilization itself. Our teaching must be clear; it must recognize the drama of the human condition, in which we all struggle with sin and in which we must all strive, with the help of grace, to embrace the good (cf. *Gaudium et Spes*, 13). Our task as teachers is to "show the inviting splendor of that truth which is Jesus Christ himself" (*Veritatis Splendor*, 83). Living the moral life involves holding fast to the very person of Jesus, partaking of his life and destiny, sharing in his free and loving obedience to the will of the Father.

May your fidelity to the Lord and the responsibility for his Church which he has given you make you personally vigilant to ensure that only sound doctrine of faith and morals is presented as Catholic teaching. Invoking the intercession of Our Lady upon your ministry, I cordially impart my Apostolic Blessing to you and to the priests, religious and lay faithful of your Dioceses.

— From the Vatican, October 2, 1998

XI

Authentic Liturgical Renewal

Dear Brother Bishops,

1. With fraternal love in the Lord I welcome you, *the Pastors of the Church in the Northwestern United States*, on the occasion of your *ad limina* visit. This series of visits by the Bishops of your country to the tombs of the Apostles Peter and Paul, and to the Successor of Peter and his collaborators in the service of the universal Church, is taking place while the whole People of God is preparing to celebrate the Great Jubilee of the Year 2000 and enter a new Christian Millennium. The two-thousandth anniversary of the Birth of the Savior is a call to all Christ's followers to seek a genuine conversion to God and a great advance in holiness. Since *the liturgy is such a central part of the Christian life*, I wish today to consider some aspects of the liturgical renewal so vigorously promoted by the Second Vatican Council as the prime agent of the wider renewal of Catholic life.

To look back over what has been done in the field of liturgical renewal in the years since the Council is, first, to see many reasons for giving heartfelt thanks and praise to the Most Holy Trinity for the marvelous awareness which has developed among the faithful of their role and responsibility in this priestly work of Christ and his Church. It is also to realize that not all changes have always and everywhere been accompanied by the necessary explanation and catechesis; as a result, in some cases there has been a misunderstanding of the very nature of the liturgy, leading to abuses, polarization, and sometimes even grave scandal. After the experience of more than thirty years of liturgical renewal, we are well placed to assess both the strengths and weaknesses of what has been done, in order more confidently to plot our course into the future which God has in mind for his cherished People.

2. The challenge now is to move beyond whatever misunderstandings there have been and to reach *the proper point of balance*, especially by entering more deeply into *the contemplative dimension of worship*, which includes the sense of awe, reverence and adoration which are fundamental attitudes in our relationship with God. This will happen only if we recognize that the liturgy has dimensions *both* local *and* universal, time-bound *and* eternal, horizontal *and* vertical, subjective *and* objective. It is precisely these tensions which give to Catholic worship its distinctive character. The universal Church is united in the one great act of praise; but it is always the worship of a particular community in a particular culture. It is the eternal worship of Heaven, but it is also steeped in time. It gathers and builds a human community, but it is also "the worship of the divine majesty" (*Sacrosanctum Concilium*, 33). It is subjective in that it depends radically upon what the worshipers bring to it; but it is objective in that it transcends them as *the priestly act of Christ himself*, to which he associates us but which ultimately does not depend upon us (*ibid.*, 7). This is why it is so important that liturgical law be respected. The

priest, who is the servant of the liturgy, not its inventor or producer, has a particular responsibility in this regard, lest he empty liturgy of its true meaning or obscure its sacred character. The core of the mystery of Christian worship is *the sacrifice of Christ offered to the Father and the work of the Risen Christ who sanctifies his People through the liturgical signs.* It is therefore essential that in seeking to enter more deeply into the contemplative depths of worship *the inexhaustible mystery of the priesthood of Jesus Christ* be fully acknowledged and respected. While all the baptized share in that one priesthood of Christ, not all share in it in the same manner. The ministerial priesthood, rooted in Apostolic Succession, confers on the ordained priest faculties and responsibilities which are different from those of the laity but which are at the service of the common priesthood and are directed at the unfolding of the baptismal grace of all Christians (cf. *Catechism of the Catholic Church*, no. 1547). The priest therefore is not just one who presides, but *one who acts in the person of Christ.*

3. Only by being radically faithful to this doctrinal foundation can we avoid one-dimensional and unilateral interpretations of the Council's teaching. The sharing of all the baptized in the one priesthood of Jesus Christ is the key to understanding the Council's call for *"full, conscious and active participation"* in the liturgy (*Sacrosanctum Concilium*, 14). *Full participation* certainly means that every member of the community has a part to play in the liturgy; and in this respect a great deal has been achieved in parishes and communities across your land. But full participation does not mean that everyone does everything, since this would lead to a *clericalizing* of the laity and a *laicizing* of the priest-

hood; and this was not what the Council had in mind. The liturgy, like the Church, is intended to be hierarchical and polyphonic, respecting *the different roles assigned by Christ* and allowing all the different voices to blend in one great hymn of praise.

Active participation certainly means that, in gesture, word, song and service, all the members of the community take part in an act of worship, which is anything but inert or passive. Yet active participation does not preclude the active passivity of *silence, stillness and listening*: indeed, it demands it. Worshipers are not passive, for instance, when listening to the readings or the homily, or following the prayers of the celebrant, and the chants and music of the liturgy. These are experiences of silence and stillness, but they are in their own way profoundly active. In a culture which neither favors nor fosters meditative quiet, the art of interior listening is learned only with difficulty. Here we see how the liturgy, though it must always be properly inculturated, must also be counter-cultural.

Conscious participation calls for the entire community to be properly instructed in the mysteries of the liturgy, lest the experience of worship degenerate into a form of ritualism. But *it does not mean a constant attempt within the liturgy itself to make the implicit explicit*, since this often leads to a verbosity and informality which are alien to the Roman Rite and end by trivializing the act of worship. Nor does it mean the suppression of all subconscious experience, which is vital in a liturgy which thrives on symbols that speak to the subconscious just as they speak to the conscious. The use of the vernacular has certainly opened up the treasures of the liturgy to all who take part, but this does not mean that the Latin language, and especially the chants which are so superbly adapted to the genius of the Roman Rite, should be wholly abandoned. If subconscious experience is ignored in worship, an affective and devotional vacuum is created and the liturgy can become not only too verbal but also too cerebral. Yet the Roman Rite is again distinctive in the balance it strikes between a spareness and a richness of emotion: *it feeds the heart and the mind, the body and the soul.*

It has been written with good reason that in the history of the Church *all true renewal has been linked to a re-reading of the Church Fathers.* And what is true in general is true of the liturgy in particular. The Fathers were pastors with a burning zeal for the task of spreading the Gospel; and therefore they were profoundly interested in all the dimensions of worship, leaving us some of the most significant and enduring texts of the Christian tradition, which are anything but the result of a barren aestheticism. The Fathers were ardent preachers, and *it is hard to imagine that there can be an effective renewal of Catholic preaching, as the Council wished, without sufficient familiarity with the Patristic tradition.* The Council promoted a move to a homiletic mode of preaching which would, like the Fathers, expound the biblical text in a way which opens its inexhaustible riches to the faithful. The importance that preaching has assumed in Catholic worship since the Council means that priests and deacons should be trained to make good use of the Bible. But this also involves familiarity with the whole Patristic, theological and moral tradition, as well as a penetrating knowledge of their communities and of society in general. Otherwise the impression is given of a teaching without roots and without the universal application inherent in the Gospel message. The excellent synthesis of the Church's doctrinal wealth contained in the *Catechism of the Catholic Church* has yet to be more widely felt as an influence on Catholic preaching.

4. It is essential to keep clearly in mind that *the liturgy is intimately linked to the Church's mission to evangelize.* If the two do not go hand in hand, both will falter. Insofar as developments in liturgical renewal are superficial or unbalanced, our energies for a new evangelization will be compromised; and insofar as our vision falls short of the new evangelization our liturgical renewal will be reduced to external and possibly unsound adaptation. The Roman Rite has always been a form of worship that looks to mission. This is why it is comparatively brief: there was much to be done outside the church; and this is why we have the dismissal *"Ite, missa est,"* which gives us the term "Mass": the community is sent forth to evangelize the world in obedience to Christ's command (cf. Matt. 28:19–20).

As Pastors, you are fully aware of the great thirst for God and the desire for prayer which people feel today. The World Youth Day in Denver stands out as evidence that the younger generation of Americans too yearns for a deep and demanding faith in Jesus Christ. They want to have an active role in the Church, and *to be sent out in the name of Christ to evangelize and transform the world around them.* Young people are ready to commit themselves to the Gospel message if it is presented in all its nobility and liberating force. They will continue to take an active part in the liturgy if they experience it as capable of leading them to a deep personal relationship with God; and it is from this experience that there will come priestly and religious vocations marked by true evangelical and missionary energy.

In this sense the young are summoning the whole Church to take the next step in implementing the vision of worship which the Council has bequeathed to us. Unburdened by the ideological agenda of an earlier time, they are able to speak simply and directly of their desire to experience God, especially in prayer both public and private. In listening to them, dear Brothers, we may well hear "what the Spirit is saying to the Churches" (Rev. 2:11).

5. In our preparation for the Great Jubilee of the Year 2000, *the year 1999 will be devoted to the Person of the Father and to the celebration of his merciful love*. Initiatives for next year should draw particular attention to the nature of the Christian life as "a great pilgrimage to the house of the Father, whose unconditional love for every human creature, and in particular for the 'prodigal son', we discover anew each day" (*Tertio Millennio Adveniente*, 49). At the core of this experience of pilgrimage is our journey as sinners into the unfathomable depths of the Church's liturgy, the liturgy of Creation, the liturgy of Heaven — all of which are in the end the worship of Jesus Christ, the Eternal Priest, in whom the Church and all creation are drawn into the life of the Most Holy Trinity, our true home. That is the purpose of all our worship and all our evangelizing.

At the very heart of the worshiping community, we find the Mother of Christ and Mother of the Church, who, from the depths of her contemplative faith, brings forth the Good News, which is Jesus Christ himself. Together with you I pray that American Catholics when they celebrate the liturgy will have in their hearts the same song that she sang: "My being proclaims the greatness of the Lord, my spirit finds joy in God my Savior. . . . God who is mighty has done great things for me, holy is his name" (Luke 1:46–50). In entrusting the priests, religious and lay faithful of your Dioceses to the Blessed Mother's loving protection, I cordially impart my Apostolic Blessing.

— *From the Vatican, October 9, 1998*

XII

Canon Law in the Life of the Church

Dear Brother Bishops,

1. With great joy I greet you, the Pastors of the Church in the States of *Colorado, Wyoming, Utah, Arizona and New Mexico.* Your *ad limina* visit, by bringing you to "see Peter" (cf. Gal. 1:18) is meant to be, in the life of the particular Churches over which you preside, an opportunity "to strengthen unity in the same faith, hope and charity, and more and more recognize and treasure that immense heritage of spiritual and moral wealth that the whole Church, joined with the Bishop of Rome by the bond of communion, has spread throughout the world" (*Pastor Bonus*, Appendix I, no. 3).

In this series of meetings with the Bishops of the United States, I have emphasized that the faithful and committed implementation of the teachings of the Second Vatican Council is the path indicated by the Holy Spirit for the whole Church to prepare for the Great Jubilee of the Year 2000 and the beginning of the new Millennium. The renewal of Christian life which was at the forefront of the Council's work is the same goal which guided Pope John XXIII to advocate *a revision of the Code of Canon Law* (cf. *Address to Roman Cardinals*, January 25, 1959), a desire reaffirmed by the Council Fathers (cf. *Christus Dominus*, 44). After much labor this revision bore fruit in the new *Code of Canon Law* promulgated in 1983 and the *Code of Canons of the Eastern Churches* promulgated in 1990. Today I wish to reflect on some aspects of your ministry in relation to the place of law in the Church.

2. The immediate purpose of the revision of the Code was to ensure that *it embodied the ecclesiology of the Second Vatican Council*. And, given that the Council's teaching aimed at stirring new energies for a new evangelization, it is clear that the revision of the Code belongs to that series of graces and gifts which the Holy Spirit has poured out so abundantly on the ecclesial community so that, in fidelity to Christ, it will enter the next Millennium seeking to give witness to the truth, to rescue and not to sit in judgment, to serve and not to be served (cf. *Tertio Millennio Adveniente*, 56).

To understand more of the link between law and evangelization we need to consider the biblical roots of law in the Church. The Old Testament insists that the Torah is the greatest of God's gifts to Israel, and each year the Jewish people still celebrate the feast called the *Rejoicing of the Torah*. The Torah is a great gift because it opens to people in every time and place the path of an ever new Exodus. For us, just as for Israel, the question is this: long ago our ancestors came forth from the slavery of Egypt, but how are we now to come forth from the slavery which afflicts us, from the Egypt of our own time and place? The biblical answer is: you will find freedom if you obey this divine Law. At the heart of biblical revelation, therefore, there lies the mystery of a liberating obedience, which reaches its supreme expression in the Crucified Christ who was "obedient unto death" (Phil. 2:8). Ultimate obedience made possible the definitive liberation of Easter.

In the Church, then, the purpose of law is the defense and promotion of the "glorious liberty of the children of God" (Rom. 8:21); this is the Good News which Christ sends us to bring to the world. To see the law as spiritually liberating runs against the grain of a certain understanding of law in Western culture, which tends to view law as a necessary evil, a kind of control required to guard fragile human rights and restrain wayward human passions, but which would disappear in the best of all possible worlds. This is not the biblical view; nor can it be the Church's view.

Authority in the Church, being a sacred ministry at the service of the proclamation of God's word and the sanctification of the faithful, can only be understood as a means for the development of the Christian life in accordance with the radical demands of the Gospel. Ecclesiastical law gives form to the community or social body of the Church, always with a view to *that supreme objective which is the salvation of souls* (cf. *Canons* 747, 978, 1752). Since this ultimate end is attained above all through the newness of life in the Spirit, the provisions of the law aim at safeguarding and fostering Christian life by regulating the exercise of faith, the sacraments, charity and ecclesiastical government.

3. The common good which the law protects and promotes is not a mere external order, but the sum of those conditions which make possible the spiritual and internal reality of *communion with God and communion between the members of the Church*. Consequently, as a basic rule, eccle-

siastical laws bind in conscience. In other words, obedience
to the law is not a mere external submission to authority
but a means of growing in faith, charity and holiness, under the guidance and by the grace of the Holy Spirit. In
this sense canon law has particular features which distin-
guish it from civil law and which preclude the application of the legal structures of civil society to the Church
without the necessary modifications. Appreciation of these
particularities is necessary in order to overcome some of
the difficulties which have arisen in recent times regarding
the understanding, interpretation and application of canon
law.

Among these particularities is *the pastoral character of
law and of the exercise of justice in the Church*. In fact, the
pastoral character of canon law is the key to the correct
understanding of *canonical equity*, that attitude of mind
and spirit which tempers the rigor of the law in order to
foster a higher good. In the Church, equity is an expression
of charity in the truth, aiming at a higher justice which
coincides with the supernatural good of the individual and
of the community. Equity, then, should characterize the
work of the pastor and the judge, who must continually
model themselves on the Good Shepherd, "consoling those
who have been struck down, guiding those who have erred,
recognizing the rights of those who have been injured, ca-
lumniated or unjustly humiliated" (Paul VI, *Address to the
Roman Rota*, February 8, 1973). Elements such as dispensa-
tion, tolerance, exempting or excusing causes, and *epikeia*,
are to be understood not as diminishing the force of law but
as complementing it, since they actually guarantee that the
law's fundamental purpose is secured. Likewise, ecclesiastical censures are not vindictive but medicinal, inasmuch

as they aim at bringing about the conversion of the sinner. *All law in the Church has truth and charity as its constitutive elements and its primary motivating principles.*

4. The Code specifies the duties of Bishops regarding the setting up of tribunals, and their activity. It is not enough to ensure that diocesan tribunals have the personnel and means to function properly. Your responsibility as Bishops — about which I encourage you to be especially vigilant — is to *ensure that diocesan tribunals exercise faithfully the ministry of truth and justice.* In my own ministry I have always felt the weight of this particular responsibility. As the Successor of Peter I have reason to be deeply grateful to my collaborators in the various tribunals of the Apostolic See: especially the Apostolic Penitentiary, the Supreme Tribunal of the Apostolic Signatura and the Tribunal of the Roman Rota, which help me in that part of my ministry which deals with the proper administration of justice.

Canon law touches on every aspect of the Church's life and therefore imposes upon Bishops a wide range of responsibilities, but it is undoubtedly in the area of marriage that these responsibilities are felt most acutely and are most complex. The *indissolubility of marriage* is a teaching that comes from Christ himself, and the first duty of pastors and pastoral workers is therefore to help couples overcome whatever difficulties arise. The referral of matrimonial cases to the tribunal should be a last resort. Great care must be taken when explaining to the faithful what a declaration of nullity is, in order to avoid the danger of its being conceived as divorce under a different name. The tribunal exercises a ministry of truth: its purpose is "to ascertain whether or not the facts exist that by natural, di-

vine or ecclesiastical law invalidate the marriage, in order
to be able to issue a true and just sentence concerning the
alleged non-existence of the marriage bond" (*Address to the
Roman Rota*, February 4, 1980, no. 2). The process leading
to a judicial decision about the alleged nullity of marriage
should demonstrate two aspects of the Church's pastoral
mission. First, it should manifest clearly the desire to be
faithful to the Lord's teaching concerning the permanent
nature of sacramental marriage. Secondly, it should be inspired by genuine pastoral concern for those who seek the
ministry of the tribunal in order to clarify their status in
the Church.

5. Justice demands that the work of tribunals be carried out conscientiously and in strict observance of canonical directions and procedures. As Moderators of your diocesan tribunals, you have the duty to ensure that the officials
of the tribunal are suitably qualified (cf. *Canons* 1420, 4;
1421, 3; 1428, 2; 1435), possessing a doctorate or at least a
licentiate in canon law. Where this is not the case, they need
to be properly dispensed by the Apostolic Signatura after
receiving specialized training for their position. In regard
to the officials of the tribunal, I urge you in particular to
see that the defender of the bond is diligent in presenting
and expounding all that can reasonably be argued against
the nullity of the marriage (cf. *Canon* 1432). Bishops whose
tribunals handle cases in second instance should ensure that
their tribunals treat their competence seriously, not acting
merely as an almost automatic confirmation of the judgment of the tribunal of first instance.

Both parties in a marriage case have rights which must
be scrupulously respected. These include the right to be

heard for the formulation of the doubt, the right to know on what grounds the case will be tried, the right to name witnesses, the right to inspect the acts, the right to know and rebut the arguments of the other party and of the defender of the bond, and to receive a copy of the final sentence. The parties are to be informed of the ways in which they may challenge the definitive sentence, including the right to appeal to the Tribunal of the Roman Rota in second instance. In regard to cases tried on the basis of psychic incapacity, that is, on the basis of some serious psychic anomaly which renders a person incapable of contracting a valid marriage (cf. *Canon* 1095), the tribunal is to make use of the services of an expert in psychology or psychiatry who shares a Christian anthropology in accordance with the Church's understanding of the human person (cf. *Address to the Roman Rota*, February 5, 1987).

A canonical process must never be seen as a mere formality to be observed or a set of rules to be manipulated. The judge may not pass sentence in favor of the nullity of a marriage if he has not first acquired the moral certainty of the existence of this nullity; probability alone is not sufficient to decide a case (cf. *ibid.*, no. 6; *Canon* 1608). Moral certainty — which is not just probability or subjective conviction — "is characterized on the positive side by the exclusion of well-founded or reasonable doubt. On the negative side, it does admit the absolute possibility of the contrary and in this it differs from absolute certainty" (Pius XII, *Address to the Roman Rota*, October 1, 1942, no. 1). Moral certainty proceeds from a multitude of indications and demonstrations which, taken separately, may not be decisive, but which taken together can exclude any reasonable doubt. If the judge cannot reach moral certainty in

the canonical trial, he must find in favor of the validity of
the matrimonial bond (cf. *Canon* 1608, 3 and 4): *marriage
enjoys the favor of the law.*

6. Dear Brother Bishops, the purpose of these brief
considerations is to encourage you in overseeing the faithful application of canonical legislation: this is essential if
the Church is to show herself ever more equal to the task
of carrying out her salvific mission (cf. Apostolic Constitution *Sacrae Disciplinae Leges*). A deeper appreciation of
the importance of canon law in the life of the Church and
the implementation of measures to guarantee a more effective and conscientious administration of justice must be
a central concern of your episcopal ministry. Fidelity to
ecclesiastical law should be a vital part of the renewal of
your particular Churches. It is a condition for unleashing
new energies for evangelization as we approach the Third
Christian Millennium. I entrust your pastoral efforts in this
regard to the maternal intercession of Mary, *Mirror of Justice*, and to you and the priests, religious and lay faithful
of your Dioceses, I gladly impart my Apostolic Blessing.

— *From the Vatican, October 16, 1998*

XIII

Towards the
Great Jubilee 2000

Dear Cardinal Law,
Dear Brother Bishops,

1. I warmly greet you, *the Bishops of New England, comprising the ecclesiastical provinces of Boston and Hartford.* During this year I have had the spiritual joy of meeting practically all the Pastors of the Church in the United States of America, representing over two hundred jurisdictions, including those of the Eastern-rite Catholic Churches. As we come to the end of this series of *ad limina* visits, I "give thanks to God always for you because of the grace which has been given you in Christ Jesus, that in every way you have been enriched in him" (cf. 1 Cor. 1:4–5). We have prayed together and listened to one another, seeking to take stock of all the good which the Holy Spirit inspires among the People of God in your country. Apart from strengthening the bonds of communion between us, these visits have enabled us to reflect, in an atmosphere of pilgrimage and prayerful calm, on the opportunities for evangelization and apostolate which lie before the Church in the United States in the light of the teaching of the Second Vatican Council and the approaching Great Jubilee of the Year 2000.

2. Occasions such as the Great Jubilee remind us of all that God has done in history, and they prompt us to look to the future, confident in the Lord's promise that he will be with us always, "to the close of the age" (Matt. 28:20). Christians know that time is neither a mere succession of days, months and years, nor a cosmic cycle of eternal return. Time is a great drama with a beginning and an end, authored and directed by God's providential care: "Within the dimension of time the world was created; within it the history of salvation unfolds, finding its culmination in the 'fullness of time' of the Incarnation, and its goal in the glorious return of the Son of God at the end of time" (*Tertio Millennio Adveniente*, 10). The Easter Vigil reminds us that the Resurrection is "the true fulcrum of history, to which the mystery of the world's origin and its final destiny leads" (*Dies Domini*, 2). *Only in the light of the Risen Christ do we come to understand the true meaning of our personal pilgrimage through time to our eternal destiny.* This is the message which the Church must proclaim today and always. She does so above all in the Liturgy, which celebrates the history of salvation and is the privileged place for our encounter with the Father and the One whom he has sent, Jesus Christ. She does so in her *kerygma* and catechesis, which make known the saving teaching of the Gospel in dialogue with the human heart's profound aspiration for something divine and eternal, something supremely good that will not slip away. And she does so in her works of charity, which seek to heal the brokenness of human lives by the healing touch of Christian love.

3. In my talks to the Bishops — addressed not only to the Bishops present on each occasion but to your en-

tire Conference — I have tried to reflect on aspects of your episcopal ministry which can open the door to the great springtime of Christianity which God is preparing as we enter the Third Christian Millennium, and of which we can already see the first signs (cf. *Redemptoris Missio*, 86). Together we have conversed about many features of the life of the Catholic community in the United States, blessed by the genuine holiness of so many of its members, marked by a deep thirst for justice, steadfast and active in all the various forms of Christian service. As Bishops you are well aware of the strengths of your people. Like the wise man of the Gospel, you must calculate how with the energies and means available you can face the urgent needs of the present time (cf. Luke 14:31). Today I believe the Lord is saying to us all: *do not hesitate, do not be afraid to engage the good fight of the faith* (cf. 1 Tim. 6:12). When we preach the liberating message of Jesus Christ we are offering *the words of life* to the world (cf. John 6:68). Our prophetic witness is an urgent and essential service not just to the Catholic community but to the whole human family. For in the Gospel the true story of the world is told, its history and its future, which is life within the communion of the Holy Trinity.

At the end of the second millennium humanity stands at a kind of crossroads. As Pastors responsible for the life of the Church, we need to meditate deeply on *the signs of a new spiritual crisis*, whose dangers are apparent not only at the personal level but regarding civilization itself (cf. *Evangelium Vitae*, 68). If this crisis deepens, utilitarianism will increasingly reduce human beings to objects for manipulation. If the moral truth revealed in the dignity of the human person does not discipline and direct the explosive energies of technology, a new era of barbarism, rather than a springtime of hope, may well follow this century of tears (cf. *Speech to the United Nations*, October 5, 1995, no. 18).

In addressing the United Nations General Assembly in 1995, I proposed that in order to recover our hope and our trust on the threshold of a new century "we must *regain sight of that transcendent horizon of possibility to which the soul of man aspires*" (*ibid.*, no. 16). Because the spiritual crisis of our times is in fact a flight from the transcendent mystery of God, it is at the same time a flight from the truth about the human person, God's noblest creation on earth. The culture of our day seeks to build without reference to the architect, ignoring the biblical warning: "Unless the Lord builds the house, those who build it labor in vain" (Ps. 127:1). In doing so, a certain part of contemporary culture misses the depth and richness of the human mystery, and life itself is thereby impoverished, being divested of meaning and joy. *No demand on our ministry is more urgent than the "new evangelization" needed to satisfy the spiritual hunger of our times.* We must not hesitate before the challenge of communicating the joy of being Christian, of being "in Christ," in the state of grace with God, and of being united with the Church. This is what can truly satisfy the human heart and its aspiration to freedom.

4.   Nowhere is the contrast between the Gospel vision and contemporary culture more obvious than in *the dramatic conflict between the culture of life and the culture of death*. I do not wish to end this series of meetings without once more thanking the Bishops for their leadership and advocacy in support of human life, particularly the lives of the most vulnerable. The Church in your country reaches

out in the defense and promotion of human life and human dignity in numerous ways. Through countless organizations and agencies she is an immensely generous provider of social services to the poor; active in support of laws more favorable to the immigrant, present in the public debate on capital punishment, aware that in the modern state the cases in which the execution of an offender is an absolute necessity are very rare, if not practically nonexistent (cf. *Evangelium Vitae*, 56; *Catechism of the Catholic Church*, no. 2267). At the same time *you rightly underscore the priority that must be given to the fundamental right to life of the unborn*, and to opposition to euthanasia and physician-assisted suicide. The witness of so many United States Catholics — including countless young people — in the service of "the Gospel of life" is a sure sign of hope for the future, and a reason for us to be thankful to the Holy Spirit who inspires so much good among the faithful.

5. In response to the spiritual crisis of our times, I am convinced that there is a radical need for *a healing of the mind as well as of the heart.* The violent history of this century is due in no small part to the closure of reason to the existence of ultimate and objective truth. The result has been a pervasive skepticism and relativism, which have not led to a more "mature" humanity but to much despair and irrationality. In the Encyclical Letter *Fides et Ratio*, published only last week, I wished to *defend the capacity of human reason to know the truth*. This confidence in reason is an integral part of the Catholic intellectual tradition, but it needs reaffirming today in the face of a widespread and doctrinaire doubt about our ability to answer the fundamental questions: Who am I? Where have I come from

and where am I going to? Why is there evil? What is there after this life? (cf. *Fides et Ratio*, 3 and 5). Many people have been led to believe that the only truths are those which can be demonstrated by experience or scientific experimentation. The result is a tendency to reduce the domain of rational inquiry to technological, instrumental, utilitarian, functional and sociological dimensions of things. A relativistic and pragmatic vision of truth has emerged. An undifferentiated plurality, based on the assumption that all positions are equally valid, replaces a legitimate pluralism of positions in dialogue (cf. *ibid*., 5). One of the most striking indications of the contemporary *lack of confidence in truth* is the tendency found among some to rest content with partial and provisional truths, "no longer seeking to ask the meaning and ultimate foundation of human, personal and social existence" (*ibid*.). By being satisfied with experimental and incomplete knowledge, reason fails to do justice to the mystery of the human person, made for the truth and deeply desirous of knowing the truth.

The consequences for the faith of this widespread attitude are serious. If reason cannot attain ultimate truths, faith loses its reasonable and intelligible character and is reduced to the realm of the non-definable, the sentimental and the irrational. The outcome is fideism. Detached from its relationship to human reason, faith loses its public and universal validity and is limited to the subjective and private sphere. In the end, theological faith is destroyed. On the basis of these concerns, I considered it important to write the Encyclical Letter *Fides et Ratio*, addressed to you, the Bishops of the Church, the principal witnesses to divine and catholic truth (cf. *Lumen Gentium*, 25). My wish is to *encourage you, as Bishops, always to keep open the horizon of your ministry, beyond the immediate tasks of your daily pastoral toil, to that deep and universal thirst for the truth which is found in every human heart.*

6.   The dialogue of the Church with contemporary culture is part of your *"diakonia* of the truth" (*Fides et Ratio*, 2). You must do all you can to raise the level of philosophical and theological reflection, not only in seminaries and Catholic institutions (cf. *ibid.*, 62), but also among Catholic intellectuals and all those who seek a deeper understanding of reality. As we approach the new millennium, the Church's defense of the human person requires a firm and open defense of the capacity of human reason to reach definitive truths concerning God, concerning man himself, concerning freedom and concerning ethical behavior. Only through reasoned reflection, open to the fundamental questions of existence and free from reductive presuppositions, can society discover sure points of reference on which to build a secure foundation for the lives of individuals and communities. Faith and reason in cooperation manifest the grandeur of the human being, "who can find fulfilment only in choosing to enter the truth, to make a home under the shade of Wisdom and dwell there" (*ibid.*, 107). The Church's long intellectual tradition is born of her confidence in the goodness of creation and the ability of reason to grasp metaphysical and moral truths. Collaboration between faith and reason, and the continued involvement of Christian thinkers in philosophy, are essential elements of the cultural and intellectual renewal that you must foster in your country.

7. In closing this series of *ad limina* visits with the American Bishops, I wish to express *my warmest personal appreciation to you for the spiritual communion, solidarity and support which you have shown me during the twenty years of my Pontificate*. I too feel that I am your friend and elder brother on the pilgrimage of faith and fidelity which together we are making in devotion to Christ and service of his Church. To the priests, religious and laity of the United States I express once more my cordial esteem and gratitude, asking the Holy Spirit to give your local Churches a new outpouring of life and energy for the mission still to be fulfilled. I pray that there will be *a continuing and all-embracing renewal of unity and love among all American Catholics, of reconciliation and mutual support in the truth of faith*. I ask God to bless your efforts in the ecumenical dialogue with other Christians, and in interreligious cooperation on the basis of the many fundamental points of contact we share with all believers. My fervent prayer is that there will be a fresh spirit of goodness, harmony and peace among all the people of the United States, so that your public life may be renewed in truthfulness and honor, and your country may carry out its historical destiny among the peoples of the world.

Commending you and your brother Bishops to the loving care of Mary Immaculate, Heavenly Patron of the United States of America, I cordially impart my Apostolic Blessing.

— From the Vatican, October 23, 1998

Basilica Press books and tapes are available
at your local Catholic bookseller.

To get a free resource catalogue of other Basilica Press
books and tapes, please contact:

Basilica Press
P.O. Box 675205
Rancho Santa Fe, CA 92067

www.basilica.com

Or call us toll-free at

888-396-2339